Daydreaming

UNLOCK

THE CREATIVE POWER

OF YOUR MIND

Daydreaming

F. Diane Barth, M.S.W.

VIKING

VIKING
Published by the Penguin Group
Penguin Books USA Inc., 375 Hudson Street,
New York, New York 10014, U.S.A.
Penguin Books Ltd, 27 Wrights Lane,
London W8 5TZ, England
Penguin Books Australia Ltd, Ringwood,
Victoria, Australia
Penguin Books Canada Ltd, 10 Alcorn Avenue,
Toronto, Ontario, Canada M4V 3B2
Penguin Books (N.Z.) Ltd, 182-190 Wairau Road,
Auckland 10, New Zealand

Penguin Books Ltd, Registered Offices:
Harmondsworth, Middlesex, England

First published in 1997 by Viking Penguin,
a division of Penguin Books USA Inc.

1   3   5   7   9   10   8   6   4   2

A NOTE TO THE READER
*The individual experiences described in this book are true. However, in order to
preserve privacy and maintain confidentiality, they are presented as composites
of more than one real person. Each portrait is the expression of combining
and synthesizing the actions and statements of a number of persons.*

LIBRARY OF CONGRESS CATALOGING IN PUBLICATION DATA
Barth, F. Diane.
Daydreaming : unlock the creative power of your mind/
F. Diane Barth.
p.   cm.
ISBN 0-670-86403-X
1. Psychoanalysis.   2. Fantasy.   3. Self-perception.   I. Title.
BF175.5.F36B37   1997
154.3—dc20   96-35885

This book is printed on acid-free paper.
∞

Printed in the United States of America
Set in Bembo
Designed by Judith Abbate

TO MY PARENTS, JOY AND GEORGE BARTH,
WITH LOVE AND GRATITUDE

ACKNOWLEDGMENTS

THIS BOOK IS one kind of daydream—a dream come true. Many people contributed to the process that allowed this to happen, and although I can never express the full extent of my gratitude, I would like to take this opportunity to thank some of them.

I am incredibly lucky to have an agent like Judith Riven, who has become a friend, mentor, guide, and much, much more, and whom I can never thank enough. I also send enormous thanks to Guy Kettelhack, who edited, supported, and taught me more than I could have imagined, and who opened a door to a new world for me. And I am deeply grateful to Mindy Werner, my editor at Viking, whose talent, hard work, and invaluable suggestions brought the book together and made this dream a reality.

Many thanks go to Roth Wilkofsky, who generously gave advice and directed me to the chain that led to Judith Riven; and to Perry Quick and my brothers Rick and David for reading and critiquing early drafts of the book. My brother David also offered indispensable suggestions and gave the book its original working title.

Many wonderful friends and special relatives have listened to me talk about my daydreams and have told me about theirs. I am grateful to everyone who has been there for me as I worked on this book, celebrating my accomplishments and commiserating and encouraging me when I felt overwhelmed and despaired that I would ever finish. To name just a few whose help and moral support were invaluable: Denise Barth, Vicki Barth, Susan Clines, Dennis Dugan, Elaine and Clarence Gunn, Rhoda and Bill Jacoby, Cynthia Medalic, Liz Ostrow, and Mimi Schade. To my parents I send loving thanks for always believing in me and encouraging me to pursue my dreams, whatever form they took.

I also thank my clients, who have shared their daydreams with me and helped me do the thinking that led to this book. I am grateful to them for allowing me to participate in their efforts to overcome difficulties and pursue their own dreams. Without their honesty and hard work, this book would not be. I am similarly grateful to the therapists I have taught and supervised, from whom I always learn much more than I teach. I thank, too, my own teachers and supervisors, as well as the members of my Monday study groups, whose support, encouragement, and discussions over our many years together have always been invaluable. To Ingrid Freidenbergs and Martin Wagner, who in their distinct personal ways taught me how to listen to and explore my own daydreams and those of my clients, I send tremendous gratitude and love.

Finally, I thank my son, Simon, and my husband, Joel, who have graciously and lovingly made so many of my dreams come true.

CONTENTS

Daydreaming

INTRODUCTION

FOR AS LONG AS I can remember, I have been a dreamer. I've always rewritten the endings of books, replayed movies in my mind, and created stories whenever I had the chance. When I was a little girl, my family took a lot of car trips—to the mountains and the beaches of North Carolina, where we lived, and to New York City to visit my grandparents. Because I was almost always carsick, I couldn't read or play games. So, during every trip, and especially the twelve-hour one to New York, I'd curl up in the back seat and amuse myself in my fantasy world.

When I began my training as a psychotherapist, I found that the fantasy world which was so natural to me was more than simple entertainment. I began to see my daydreams as powerful tools, a valuable means of gaining self-knowledge. I realized that my daydreams were a constant, ongoing source of information about myself—my beliefs, dreams, fears—which illuminated a good deal about the choices I've made and the ways I view myself and other people. At first I was convinced that this world of daydreams was peculiar to me. Its lessons seemed too idiosyncratic to apply to my clients. This suspicion appeared to be corroborated by the lack of attention daydreams had received from the psychoanalytic and therapeutic community. Whereas there was a vast psychoanalytic literature on what was called "unconscious" fantasy (meaning, I have since come to understand, daydreams that you don't know you're having) and on dreams remembered from sleep, very few therapists were writing or talking about the very personal, conscious thoughts and images of daydreams. (Interestingly, the first professional article I have ever seen that addresses this absence of therapeutic interest in daydreams appeared in the *Journal of the American Psychoanalytic Association* in the summer of 1996, while I was working on this book.)

My clients dismissed their own daydreams most of the time as light fun or a waste of time. If they thought or spoke about them at all, they took them literally, as something that had to be put into action to have any "real" meaning. For example, one woman who daydreamed about being a prima ballerina felt embarrassed by these thoughts, which she saw as nothing more than the vestige of an old, childish wish. It didn't occur to her to examine the daydream for any other meaning. She simply brushed it aside as silly and unrealistic—an unhelpful distraction, unrelated to the business of "real life."

However, more and more, I discovered amazing gems of information in my clients' briefly mentioned daydreams. Those seemingly insignificant thoughts that occurred as they made their children's lunches or drove to the supermarket, as they worked at their desks or sat in meetings, contained important details about themselves—details that had the potential to teach them a great deal about who they were, what they feared, and what they most desired. I began, tentatively at first, to probe a bit, to ask about

F

these passing thoughts and images that popped up continually in my clients' lives. To my delight, the response was often enthusiastic and always fascinating. People who had once quickly dismissed their daydreams became grateful for the permission to explore them. Soon, talking about and exploring daydreams became an essential tool in my practice.

Since that time, I have presented my findings and speculations about daydreams in numerous workshops with consistently exciting results. Therapists and clients alike have discovered that daydreams have a value and power equal to night dreams. They are as "royal" a "road to the unconscious" (to use Freud's phrase) as dreams remembered from sleep, but in many ways more accessible, since they occur while we are awake and our minds are more alert.

In *Daydreaming* I have drawn on published research as well as explorations of daydreams I've made, together with my clients and in consultation with other therapists, to develop a guide that will help *you* to examine these fascinating nuggets of information in your own life.

This book will help you learn to pay attention to your daydreams in a new way. You'll find, first of all, that every daydream is your own creation—the condensed, frequently symbolic product of your own imagination. You daydream for a variety of reasons: sometimes, obviously, to make plans and set goals for the near and distant future; but also to distract yourself from uncomfortable feelings, to make yourself happy, to work through difficult situations, and much more.

Your daydreams are scripts that you write. You will discover not only how they can enhance your psychological and emotional well-being, but how to *read* your daydream tales for their symbolic and personal meaning: to find out more about yourself. As you begin to understand your daydreams—why you created a particular one and why you began to think about it when you did—

you will gain new and powerful insight into how you construct your own experience. The more you understand about yourself, the more choices you will realize are open to you. You will increase your ability to alter your decisions—the small ones and the large ones. And the more you do, the more you will be able to make your life move in the direction you want.

Prepare yourself for an extraordinary odyssey—sometimes enchanting, sometimes disturbing, but always enlightening. You are telling yourself more than you know, many times a day. This book will help you to sort out these messages and to make use of them to create a richer, freer, and more satisfying life.

Part One

CHAPTER ONE

Chinese Boxes:
What Is a Daydream?

DAYDREAMS, LIKE NIGHT DREAMS, are experienced differently by each of us. You may enjoy yours, whereas your best friend worries about or is distracted by his. But perhaps you are not even sure what we mean by "daydreams," and you wonder if you have them at all.

This question is not surprising. Daydreams are elusive entities, hard to pin down and equally hard to define. According to Dr. Jerome Singer, a psychologist at Yale University and a pioneer in the study of mental imagery, one of the problems is that there is no general agreement on exactly what a daydream is. He suggests that daydreams are personal reveries, internal monologues, or fantasies (which to my mind is just a fancy name for daydreams). According to Dr. Singer, daydreams generally involve a shift away from something that we're trying to focus on in the outside world and toward some private responses to something going on inside of us. Dr. Singer tells us that daydreams can be "pictures in the mind's eye," memories of the past or ideas about the future, awareness of our bodily sensations and our emotions, and "those little inner voices we hear talking to us somewhere in our heads."

Daydreams can be highly changeable, making dramatic shifts throughout your life—even throughout a single day. In the morning, you may daydream about meeting the perfect man; by dinner, you may imagine being an independent woman who doesn't need a man. Both the content and the meaning of daydreams can change, continually, kaleidoscopically, from one moment to the next. Yet—to add to the confusion—some daydreams go basically unaltered for years, apparently untouched by passing time. A daydream can be a brief, practical thought—"Buy milk on the way home tonight"—or a long involved fantasy with no connection to your daily life. It can appear once, twice, several times, and then disappear; or it can occur repeatedly, even obsessively.

You may be wondering which type of daydream is more significant—which would be more useful to analyze. There is no simple answer to this question, because daydreams don't always signal their importance in obvious ways. A long drawn-out or recurring fantasy is not necessarily more meaningful than a brief internal reminder to pick up the dry-cleaning. So how do you choose what daydreams to pursue? First, simply choose a daydream that *interests* you. Every daydream is your psyche's attempt to redirect your attention from a task or an activity in the outside world to something going on internally; thus every daydream will have some information of value to you. Even when it seems to be a waste of time or a distraction, even when it seems simple and straightforward, a daydream is like a Chinese box: inside each box is another, each packed with symbols whose meanings, once decoded, can provide you with precious data about your internal world. But don't worry that you have to analyze *all* of your daydreams. (If you did, you'd never have time for anything else.) A few that pique your curiosity, even if they are selected randomly, will lead you right into that interior space.

Like the dreams we have while we're asleep, daydreams are divorced from physical action. In other words, you usually cannot act on a daydream in the moment, although it may direct you to future action. Even plans for real activities are daydreams—thoughts and images of actions you are *going* to take, rather than something you are doing in the here and now.

Your daydreams may take you by surprise, appearing without warning while your mind is idling or you are thinking about something else. Or you may plan your private time, making room and opportunity to savor these fantasies. Though they often take the form of visual images, daydreams can also appear in words, music, or other sounds, as well as through other bodily senses—touch, taste, smell. A taste of watermelon on a hot summer day, for example, can spontaneously summon memories of childhood picnics in the backyard. These sensations are not always fully developed daydreams, but they are tip-offs to internal monologues that you haven't verbalized, even to yourself. For example, a snatch of a song running through your head may signal a daydream—a wish captured by the lyrics, an image of the night you and your boyfriend decided it was "your" song, or your own dream of becoming a singer.

When you reflect on a daydream, you may know exactly what triggered it—a whiff of bread from a bakery may send you instantly to your grandmother's kitchen. But you may also have no idea where it came from. It may seem as though it just dropped into your mind out of the stratosphere, with no connection to any experience you can think of. However, even these "stratospheric" daydreams are your creation: symbolic messages from your own psyche.

How do you begin to explore and understand these messages and eventually make use of them? First by giving yourself permission and time to pay attention to your daydreams—to *catch* them as they fly by, to look at them, and to heed the feelings and thoughts they bring with them.

It's a good idea to do the exercises described here in a notebook that you keep exclusively for your daydreams. From time to time, write down a daydream that seems particularly interesting or puzzling, and note both the context (where and when you had the daydream) and also the three or four thoughts that immediately follow this internal monologue. You will find it useful at times to turn back to these notes—to jog your memory, stimulate other associations, even just to remind yourself that you feel more than one way about a certain person, event, or situation. This will help to keep your perspective wider and more open—understanding that feelings change, that the "self" you were one day is different from the "self" you are today. You'll also discover, as you pay close attention to the details of various daydreams and the thoughts that follow them, some of the stories you tell yourself over and over.

CATCHING YOUR
DAYDREAMS

In your daydream notebook write down the next three daydreams you notice. They don't have to be significant ones. Nor should you write a major treatise on any of them—just a few words or phrases will be sufficient. All you want to do is briefly note the daydream images.

Here are some examples of what I mean:

1. Can't wait for summer. Cool, green mountains, away from the dirt and heat of the city; reading a book under a tree; kids in camp; peace and quiet.

2. Thought about taking the dog to the vet. This is a daydream? She hates going to the vet—dread trying to get her in the car. Thoughts go to giving her a bath—equally difficult. Should have the vet give her bath—kill two birds with one stone.

3. Just before I turned out the light to go to sleep, imagined winning the lottery. All my troubles over. Pay debts, buy everything I want, take care of my old age . . .

That's all. Later we'll talk about the significance of when and where a daydream takes place, and we'll look at other tools that can help you glean information from your daydreams. But simply by describing your images in this straightforward way, you've taken the crucial first step in analyzing these fantasies: putting them into words.

DAYDREAMS: THEIR FORM AND FUNCTION

Even if you are very aware of your daydreams, you probably don't realize how much time you actually spend on them. According to the innovative work of Dr. Eric Klinger, another pioneer in the study of daydreams, these personal reveries may occupy as much as 30–40 percent of our waking time, each daydream generally lasting between five and fourteen seconds. If this comes as a surprise, it certainly offers clear evidence of how automatically you have learned to dismiss, ignore, or forget these frequent visitors. But it also implies that daydreams must have a *purpose:* why else would we resort to them so often?

Indeed, they do have a purpose—many purposes, in fact. Your daydreams are a means of coping with painful experiences. By reminding you of good times, offering you hope, and suggesting alternatives in difficult situations, they help you soothe and calm yourself when you're hurt, upset, or frightened. They allow you to see yourself acting in situations where action is impossible, to take revenge in your thoughts when actual revenge would be unwise or completely out of the question (like telling your boss what you *really* think of her), to solve the unsolvable, to turn bad into good. Even when they seem bizarre (you see yourself as a superhero, flying through the sky, or as Cleopatra, Napoleon, or Dorothy in Oz), your fantasies can enhance your self-esteem or boost you out of a bad mood. They can comfort you, provide necessary rest and relaxation, offer escape from a situation you find intolerable, act as tools for creative work.

In his early research on daydreams, Dr. Singer discovered that children who daydream are often happier and more cooperative and have longer attention spans than children who do not. Dr. Klinger and his colleagues at the University of Minnesota learned that all of our daydreams (even bad ones) can perform important functions, such as problem-solving, relaxation, and the enhancement of self-esteem. And Dr. Stephen Gold, a psychologist at Northern Illinois University, found that you can reduce depression by paying attention to—savoring and remembering—your pleasant daydreams. The research done by Dr. Gold and his colleagues also showed that these personal reveries provide an opportunity for rehearsing or planning upcoming events, as well as increasing arousal and providing novelty. In other words, among other things, daydreams keep us from being bored.

Of course, not all daydreams are pleasant. Some of them turn good feelings into bad. They can take away hope, make you feel terrible, lower your self-esteem. They can hurt—sometimes to the point of interfering with "real" life. What beneficial function could these dark dreams possibly have? Frequently, bad or negative daydreams are your way of attempting to make peace with a painful experience, or the fear of one. In daydreams we "try out" not only our positive wishes and hopes, but our worst-case scenarios as well, in the attempt to inure ourselves to them, to practice *tolerating* what might go wrong. "Bad" daydreams can be the psyche's attempt to undo a traumatic experience, or to deal with intolerable or inexpressible feelings—to gain mastery over a terrible event (past or imagined) by reliving and surviving it.

When my son was five, he, my husband, and I were caught in a freak tornado in western Massachusetts. It was a terrifying experience for all of us. Rain and hail pelted the car with a fury, forcing us to stop. Flying debris crashed into us from all sides, smashing the windows, denting and scraping the doors, hood, trunk, and sides of the car. The winds swirling around us threatened to hurl the car into the air. The few moments it lasted seemed to go on for an eternity.

The damage and destruction left in its wake were imprinted permanently in our memories. We were extremely lucky—apart from a good deal of damage to the car, we were unharmed. However, for many weeks afterward, the experience haunted each of us in our daydreams. A rattling window or a gust of wind would elicit an anxious inquiry from my son—"How do tornadoes happen? What happened to the car? Could we have been picked up and thrown around? Could we have been killed?"—which seemed to indicate some of his daydreams. My own daydreams would unexpectedly recur with a chance thought about the car, or when a cloud suddenly covered the sun. I would find myself visualizing the sudden deluge of rain and hail, the wind and debris, the destroyed buildings and cars, the downed power lines, overturned vehicles, and uprooted trees, reliving the horror over and over. My husband had a similar set of flashbacks—a common reaction to trauma of this sort.

Why does this happen? Isn't it simply self-torture? Why would we keep putting ourselves through such a terrible experience? In fact, these daydreams were adaptive attempts to process our terror—to make it manageable, eventually to overcome it. They helped us sift through our experience as a necessary stage in the task of moving beyond it.

Sometimes trauma relived in daydreams is so powerful and so frightening that it "sticks," and doesn't go away after doing its duty in the process of self-healing. Later on you'll learn how to deal with "stuck" daydreams, how to move through and beyond them. But right now it's enough to understand that terrifying daydreams do have a function. Far from merely scaring the wits out of you, they are part of your continuing effort to cope with your fears and gain mastery over them.

One of the most important things to understand about daydreams is that, like night dreams, they are symbolic—sometimes in very baffling ways. Remember the woman who daydreamed of being a prima ballerina? At first she thought she was simply reliving an old childhood wish. To some extent, this was true. But when she examined the feelings that the daydream called up, she realized that she was longing for something—not perhaps to become a ballerina, but to have the grace, beauty, artistry, and lightness she associated with being a ballerina. She felt weighted down by the drudgery of a job that bored her. Pirouetting gracefully across the stage was a symbol to her of a freedom that she longed for—a freedom that, as she began to explore and accept her hunger for it, she began to realize she might achieve in her life in a variety of ways besides becoming a ballerina.

Symbols can be obscure, but we make use of them all the time, and not only in daydreams. In this book, you'll learn how to "read" the coded messages in your daydreams. This isn't as simple as offering a black-and-white guide to "common daydream symbols and what they mean." No matter how they were formed—whether they are based on memories, stories your parents told you, books you have read, movies you have seen, songs you have heard, or your own private imaginings—in your daydreams you form your *own* symbols and stories. They have specific meaning for *you*. A blue car, for example, may mean one thing in your daydream and something quite different in your next-door neighbor's.

No one can make you daydream or tell you what to daydream about. And no one can interpret your daydreams without knowing you—very, very well. Ultimately, it's up to you to decide what the meanings of those symbols and stories might be.

YOUR OWN PRIVATE IDAHO: TEASING OUT THE MEANINGS OF A DAYDREAM

How do we "tease out" the symbolic meanings of our daydreams and learn from them? Here's an example.

Michael, a well-traveled and successful businessman in his mid-fifties, attended a dinner party with friends and found himself daydreaming of being in Paris. As a young man, he had often traveled to Europe, and he had ever since dreamed of moving to Paris, his favorite city in the world. Now, as a middle-aged man with family and business concerns, he found it harder to take the kinds of trips he had enjoyed so much in his youth. Yet, although it was certainly unlikely that he would move to Paris at this point, he continued to imagine doing just that.

Michael came to me because he felt that something was missing in his life, and this disturbed and puzzled him.

"What have I got to complain about?" he asked me at our first meeting. "I have a good marriage. My kids are normal teenagers—not perfect by any means, but good kids." And his business had been successful beyond his wildest hopes. But somehow all of this good fortune wasn't enough. In his mind, Michael kept drifting back, again and again, to Paris.

At the dinner party, he had drifted away more completely than he had in a long time. This unnerved and embarrassed him. As his friends chatted away about an art exhibit they'd all been to (which he hadn't seen, or even heard of), he imagined himself at a wonderful little bistro on the Left Bank. He could taste the *blanquette de veau* and the crisp white wine. He could feel the warm humid air on his face and hear voices speaking rapid French all around him. Suddenly, the friend sitting next to him in "reality" jabbed him with an elbow. "What do you think about it, Michael?" Michael was still four thousand miles away. He had no idea what conversation his companions were having back in the U.S.A. He could only tell you about the ones he overheard in that Left Bank bistro. . . .

At first, Michael didn't think this recurring Parisian daydream had any surprising meaning: he just missed Paris. But I thought there might be more to this fantasy, which had interfered with his ability to be present in the here and now. It suggested that something significant was going on inside him; the daydream could be a valuable source of information. I asked Michael to give me more details, as many as he could summon up.

"I don't know how much detail I can give you," he began. "It's pretty simple. I see myself living in a fourth- or fifth-floor walk-up on the Left Bank. I think it would have been great to live back in Hemingway's time, the 1920s. I'd have loved to be in Paris during the heyday of all those American artists and writers, hanging on to Gertrude Stein's every word. It must have been really magical then. But for some reason, my daydream isn't about living there in the 1920s—it's now, not then. The apartment is dark, small, basic. No luxuries. I don't have a lot of money. But it has windows opening out onto the street, and I imagine myself waking up in the morning, making myself a cup of café au lait, standing at my window as I drink it."

"What do you see out the window?"

"People walking to work with that firm, focused stride that Parisians have—solid, not running two inches off the ground, like New Yorkers do."

Then I asked Michael a key question in any daydream analysis: "How do you feel in the daydream?"

"Happy. Grounded. Connected to myself." Michael paused for a moment, considering. "I wish I could feel that way in my real life." He hesitated again. "I just thought of something funny—well, not funny, really: strange, I guess I should say. It doesn't seem to have anything to do with what I'm talking about."

I asked him to tell me about it anyway, since such unrelated thoughts are often significant.

"Well, I grounded my sixteen-year-old daughter—Suzanne—this past weekend. She'd stayed out past her curfew one too many times. She's a good kid, basically—but she's been hanging out with some kids I'm not crazy about, and I'm worried about their influence on her." He was silent for a few moments. "*Kids* these days. Remember that old song—'What's the matter with kids today?' I guess that's been the eternal cry of parents. I was thinking of myself as a nineteen-year-old kid—so full of myself, thought the world was my oyster. But I was a good kid. Worked incredibly hard—my family didn't have much money, and I managed to get myself a scholarship to Yale. A history teacher in high school helped me—it was wonderful, the way he believed in me. I owe him a lot. But I take some credit myself. I've spent my whole life working hard, doing what needed to be done." Michael stopped short. "Sorry," he said. "I'm off the track."

"I don't know that you *are* off the track," I said. "Keep going wherever your thoughts lead you."

Like most people, Michael had difficulty following his random images. He was so used to keeping his thoughts "on track" that he instantly rejected those apparently disconnected, illogical threads of thought that therapists call "associations." But in the loose threads were crucial ties to the hidden meanings of his daydreams.

In this instance, Michael had not yet completely rejected the thought but was still a little uncomfortable about pursuing it. "I don't see that it's important," he said. "And, besides, it's kind of embarrassing."

I reassured Michael that it was normal to be embarrassed by some of his daydream associations. After all, if we were comfortable with these unknown aspects of ourselves, we wouldn't need to keep them hidden. I asked him to try to put into words *why* the thoughts he had just noticed were embarrassing, without talking about what he was embarrassed by. "Oh, I guess I like to think of myself as modest, not conceited. And these thoughts make me sound the opposite—conceited, full of myself—images I don't like."

Once he had verbalized his reluctance, Michael discovered that it was easier to talk about the embarrassing thoughts.

"It's just . . . I don't know where that cocky, hopeful kid

went. I mean, I've got a lot to be proud of. I'm very glad about my success, even if I had to bust my you-know-what to achieve it. I came from very little, and I've managed to achieve a lot. And that trip to Paris—hell, I'd just aced Yale, and I decided to reward myself, do whatever I wanted to do! You could get to Europe cheap then. It was *incredible*—but it was so brief. The end of the summer, I was back in the States, in grad school, on scholarship again. I mean, I had a lot to be proud of—what I did with the opportunities I had. . . .

"Don't get me wrong. I *do* feel pretty good about what I've done with my life. I own my own business, have a great family. Suzie, like I told you, is basically a good kid. But those boys she hangs out with . . ." Michael paused for a moment, then blushed a little. "Well, I was going to tell you how full of themselves they are, how obnoxious and cocky and disrespectful. But after what I was saying a minute ago, it's not hard to see that I'm *jealous* of those young guys. They make me feel like it's all over for me. They're so arrogant. They've got energy, expectations. . . ."

Another moment of silence. I asked Michael if he could say what he was thinking about.

"Well," he started, "it's hard being at this place in my life. So much of it seems *over.* It's all ahead for Suzie and her crowd. . . . So I guess I escape—to Paris. To that moment—it feels like the only moment I ever knew—of being free and self-confident and sophisticated and powerful. Is there anything more wonderful than being a smart young man in Paris?"

The Paris of Michael's daydream turned out to be a potent and complicated symbol for him. It represented youthful hope, promise, and excitement, as well as some of the sad and deflated feelings he had just acknowledged. But he also lost himself in the daydream to escape emotions he found unacceptable, like his jealousy of his daughter Suzie's young male friends, for example. For Michael, acknowledging his competitive feelings with these boys meant feeling bad about himself in many different ways. But because the feelings were there yet not recognized, he was left with a painful sense of "something missing."

What was missing was both his lost youth and a clear, satisfying sense of who he was today. His daydream of living in Paris was an unconscious attempt to bring back that lost youthful part of himself, and at the same time to soothe himself for not being that young man now. I asked Michael if he had had any of these feelings when he "checked out" of the dinner party.

He nodded. "I didn't think about it then, but, looking back, I can see that I felt out of place and inferior all of a sudden. These are my friends, and I know they like and respect me. But they were talking about some art exhibit at the Museum of Modern Art, something I didn't know anything about. I guess I was feeling stupid. So I escaped to Paris to prove to myself I wasn't some country rube. I've spent time there, I can speak French. *I* was 'somebody,' too. . . ."

Michael could not change the fact that he was in his fifties, nor the fact that his daughter was growing up. Both these realities fed his feelings of depression and sadness (for which the feeling that "something is missing" was also a code). But now that he'd managed to look at some of these emotions, he felt more capable of coping with them; and as a result, he also felt freer to make some new decisions. He began to think about looking for something new and achievable to do, something he could feel hopeful and alive about.

Michael's associative journey as he reflected on his Parisian daydream may seem a bit circuitous—but that is precisely the point. By following this roundabout voyage into his internal world, Michael had discovered how richly condensed a symbol Paris was for him. It represented hope and loss, success and failure. It taught him something more about the nature of the "something missing" he'd complained of feeling when he first walked into my office. Understanding what the daydream meant took some work, but it also freed him up to move forward in his life. And it's the kind of work we can all learn to do.

MAKING SPACE: THE FIRST STEPS IN DAYDREAM ANALYSIS

You can follow the same process that Michael did to analyze your own daydreams. You have already begun to heed your daydreams, to catch them as they fly across your thoughts. From time to time, choose one of these daydreams and put it into words. Even better, write it down in your daydream diary. Note as many of the details of the dream as you can. Write them down, too. Later, we'll talk more about what you do with these "daydream elements." Right now it's just important that you're starting to notice them.

Pay attention to the context—that is, the specific time and place—in which the daydream appears. Observe your specific mood and thoughts, as well as the general issues in your life at that moment. As you think about the dream, try to notice any other thoughts, images, or ideas that occur to you, even if they seem random or off track. These thoughts may turn out to take you right to the heart of your daydreams.

Michael was able to follow his associations and learn from them because he gradually learned not to cut them off. Our own daydreams may remain mute to us if we don't allow ourselves to pay attention to them—to seemingly insignificant, silly, or routine details in them; to odd or confusing or embarrassing feelings and sensual impressions they evoke in us; to seemingly wild or offbeat thoughts that emerge. Michael didn't know at first why he found himself thinking of "grounding" his daughter Suzanne. The reason for this association only became clear to him later, as he allowed himself to follow the train of thoughts, memories, and feelings leading first from the daydream itself and then from his feelings about his daughter and her friends and their youthful cockiness.

You may find, as Michael did, that some of your thoughts and feelings embarrass you; but you may also find that just acknowledging your discomfort, anxiety, or embarrassment can make it easier to explore your thoughts. The crucial thing is to make plenty of space for whatever comes to your mind as you begin this work.

Once again, you see that it isn't a matter of decoding a symbol in any simplistic, follow-the-numbers way. There are no black-and-white equations here. The symbols in our daydreams, like symbols in night dreams, are condensations of our hopes and fears, loves and hates, wishes and needs. They may, and often do, have both "positive" and "negative" elements.

You may be thinking, "Yeah, but Michael had a therapist to help him." It's true that sometimes a therapist can help coax associations from a daydream. But you can learn to "self-coax." It takes time and practice—admittedly, a kind of practice many of us aren't used to. Most of us are couch potatoes when it comes to fantasies: if we have a fleeting daydream, we rarely allow ourselves to notice it, much less follow a train of associations from it. The rest of this book will show you how to tease out what such daydreams have to tell you.

Obviously, I'm not talking about analyzing every daydream. But when you choose a daydream—either because it is troublesome, or interesting, or because you just can't get it out of your mind—there are some basic questions that you can ask yourself. These questions, like those I asked Michael, will help move your thoughts and associations along the path of self-awareness.

FLEXING YOUR
FANTASY MUSCLES

Select a daydream—any daydream that you think of. It can be one that's just come to your mind, or one that you have regularly; it can be one of the daydreams you described in the earlier exercise. Now ask yourself the following questions:

1. Where were you and what were you doing when you had the daydream? What were you thinking about just before you had it?

Betty, for example, decided to analyze a brief, passing daydream about buying milk. The daydream interested her for two reasons: she couldn't understand why she remembered that she needed milk while she was in a meeting and couldn't do anything about it, and she couldn't figure out why she forgot to stop when she passed right by the grocery store on her way home that night.

As she thought back about the moment when the reminder to buy milk drifted through her head, Betty remembered only that she was bored in the meeting. But then she recalled that she had begun to daydream about her upcoming long weekend trip to visit some friends in the mountains.

2. How do you (or the main character of the fantasy) feel *in* the daydream?

If you recognize some difficult feelings in a daydream, ask yourself if you had any of those feelings as you started to have the daydream. They may lead directly to the meaning of your daydream.

Unlike Michael, who felt self-confident and cocky in his Paris daydream and insecure just before noticing it, Betty had no apparent feelings in her brief reverie on milk. But she did have some feelings about her holiday weekend. She was anticipating the visit to the mountains with pleasure. She was also feeling guilty about leaving Mathilda, her cat, alone for three days.

3. What comes to your mind in relation to these feelings?

Betty said that she had relieved her boredom in the meeting by daydreaming about her upcoming trip. Unfortunately, these fantasies reminded her that she was leaving Mathilda alone, and her discomfort about doing so marred the pleasure of imagining her long weekend. She had planned to assuage her guilt by giving the cat milk as a special treat; but now it occurred to her that by forgetting the milk she might have been sending herself another message. It was as if she were saying, "You can't get off the hook so easily."

Like everything about daydream analysis, these questions are deceptively simple; the answers will not be so easy. Allow yourself time and space to wonder about them; don't feel that you have to know everything immediately. Like Betty, you may find the answers leading to other daydreams that are threaded around and through the one you first noticed. Each daydream will provide you with more information. Just keep asking yourself these questions and letting the answers open up tiny new spaces in your internal world. But keep in mind that the process of learning to understand the meanings of your daydreams will not happen overnight. Slowly you will find your daydreams opening up—and you will discover yourself in new territory.

That territory is what I'll help you to explore next: the stories your daydreams hide, the stories they can tell you. They are often complex, contradictory, and frequently more directly related to your daily life than you may think. They can tell you a surprising amount about what you think of yourself, your family, friends, colleagues, and the world you live in.

Be forewarned: These stories are also often baffling—and sometimes exasperating—because you can virtually count on their being incomplete. Pieces are often missing; meanings are often hidden or distorted. Like Alice in Wonderland, you must make sense out of a world where nothing is as it seems. In fact, interpreting your daydreams is a lot like doing a jigsaw puzzle—but one whose pieces change, or disappear and reappear like the grin of the Cheshire Cat. Yet, in the process of finding the pieces and making sense of them, you are also growing and changing. As you grow and change, you will understand more about the stories you tell yourself, even as you discover that you are already telling yourself new ones.

Sound a bit confusing, even forbidding? That's Wonderland for you. But the discoveries that await you promise to make the journey more than worthwhile.

Read on—and find out for yourself.

CHAPTER TWO

Breaking the Code: Understanding the Symbols in Your Daydreams

THE STORIES THAT make up our daydreams—whether they're whole or in fragments—offer us potent information about ourselves, significant clues to our deepest dreams and desires. In fact, identity itself may *depend* on telling ourselves these "stories." As Joan Didion writes in her essay "The White Album," "We tell ourselves stories in order to live." These tales that spring so organically out of our imaginations enable us to make sense not only of our feelings, past and present, but also of the world around us.

However, as we've already seen, the *meanings* of the stories we create aren't always immediately visible to us. Learning from, and learning to use, our daydreams—bringing to awareness the hidden meanings that fuel the symbols our daydreams continually offer us—requires some decoding. Sometimes we don't even think to question our stories. They may just seem to be "true," obvious, beyond argument. Let's say you've always daydreamed about a strong, silent, powerful, kind man who understands you on a level deeper than words, a man to whom you can tell everything, who will love you and give you the comfortable, secure life you yearn for. There are several stories in this daydream. The comforting, hope-filled fantasy is obvious; but this tale also offers some vital clues to the stories you tell yourself—your assumptions—about men and love and security. But it also contains symbols that represent your unconscious beliefs about yourself. You may be conscious that you're comparing Harvey or Dan or Pete with this ideal daydream man in your head, but do you realize that you're also measuring yourself against a related image of what you think of as "womanly" and "happy"?

We all have unquestioned (and sometimes unconscious) models which give order to our waking life and provide a means of assessing ourselves as well as other people and events. As Joan Didion suggests, we may depend on the stories implied by these models to *survive*—certainly to give us direction. But many of the stories we tell ourselves are based on old—sometimes childhood—beliefs that we don't think to question. We just go on accepting them as true, even though they no longer make sense from our adult point of view. They are what Dr. Roy Schafer, a psychologist in New York City, has called "organizing stories"—assumptions we make about ourselves and other people that color everything we do and think. These unexamined scripts help give a kind of cohesiveness to our lives, but they can also close off alternatives and limit our options. Decoding the stories, examining the beliefs they perpetuate, widens our range of possibilities.

Michael, in the last chapter, is a good example of someone who has managed to decipher his daydreams. Let's consider some other examples, and as we go along, we'll extract some principles that you can apply to your own daydreams.

LESSONS OF A DAYDREAM DIARY: EXPLORING "THE UNTHOUGHT KNOWN"

When I first met Jon, he was badly stuck in a series of obsessive, repeated daydreams. All he could think about was Tracy, his ex-girlfriend. The end of the relationship had been traumatic for him, and although he "knew" there were good reasons for it to be over, he missed Tracy and could not stop thinking about how much he loved her. He thought about her first thing when he woke up in the morning, and he thought about her last thing before he went to bed. He even dreamed about her while he slept. He could not concentrate at work, because his thoughts kept turning to Tracy. He told me he wanted "some kind of resolution of this obsession." He hoped he'd be able to put her out of his mind and move on. He had ended the relationship himself, because of what, rationally, he still believed were insurmountable personality conflicts. Tracy and he were like oil and water. By the end, they couldn't seem to be together for five minutes without fighting. So why couldn't he get her out of his mind, especially since he had all the evidence he needed that their relationship could never work?

I explained to Jon that he was probably stuck in these daydreams because he wasn't getting whatever messages he was trying to communicate to himself through them. I suggested that, rather than fight his feelings, he might want to give himself permission for a while to pay more attention to them as well as any thoughts that were disturbing him. I recommended that he keep a day-dream diary. In it I asked him to make a brief note each time he thought about Tracy. Just the time of day, and a word or two about the thought or image or other sensory impression, e.g.: "9 a.m.—thought I heard her voice," or "Noon—wonder what she's doing," or "Midnight—thinking of her skin, what it felt like when we made love." If he wanted to, he could add more details, including more specifics about the daydream itself and also where he was, what he was doing, and how he was feeling just before he noticed that he was thinking about her.

Jon was afraid he would spend all of his time writing about Tracy; one of his goals, he said, was to get her *out* of his mind, not to think more about her. But he was interested when I told him that, if he could bear with the process for a while, we might learn something important not only about how he could resolve the relationship with Tracy, but also about why he was having so much trouble doing so.

If you, like Jon, are stuck in a daydream, it would be a good idea for you to start a daydream diary, too. Then, as you read about Jon, try asking yourself the questions I asked him, and writing the answers in your diary. Later in this section there is an exercise that will help you analyze the meaning of the messages you are sending yourself—in code—in these repeated, unchang-ing daydreams.

After he had kept a record of his daydreams about Tracy for a week, Jon came back to discuss them with me. I asked him if he saw any patterns in them. "Only that a lot of them are about physical sensations," he told me. We also noticed that they fre-quently occurred during "down time"—that is, when he was taking a shower, getting ready for bed, waking up, eating alone. This is not unusual: it is common to notice your daydreams more when you have free time. For this reason, it's important to give yourself an opportunity to relax when you are trying to interpret your daydreams. On the other hand, for the same reason, people often encourage you (or you may encourage yourself) to "keep busy, get your mind off it," when you're obsessing about something unpleasant or worrisome. The idea is that, if you don't have time to notice your thoughts, the unpleasant concern will go away. Sometimes distracting yourself works. It can give you a chance to create new daydreams to help you work through the problems that caused the obsessive thoughts in the first place. But when a concern keeps popping up, like a cork under water, your daydreams can be a valuable tool for finding a better solution.

Jon's daydreams were not kept at bay by work or play. Whatever he was doing, wherever he was, he could suddenly find himself wandering through a fantasy about Tracy. Since daydreams are as multifaceted as diamonds, I am always curious when someone comes in with dreams as single-minded as Jon's of Tracy. I wonder where the other images might be, and why they are being kept out of the picture. Not that this suppression of ideas is a conscious process (unless, at first, the other stories just seem too embarrassing to report). There is always a good reason for the omission, often related to feelings that come up with the story, and that are frightening or disturbing or overwhelming and therefore have to be kept out of sight.

As I explained to Jon, the best way to find out about the unknown stories and pictures and the feelings they represent is to start with what you already know. Pay attention to the images that occur to you, the voices you hear, the stories you see. Through these conscious thoughts and impressions you will open the door to a chain of associations. The thought sequence that follows may seem totally unrelated to the daydreams that call them up (as we saw with Michael, who, to his initial confusion, found his associations moving from Paris to his anxieties about his daughter), but the links will eventually lead you to some of those underlying assumptions and beliefs that we've been talking about. We drop clues to the mystery of our hidden stories every time we think and talk about our daydreams. The task is to collect these clues (like the feelings you gathered in the last exercise) and gradually put them together to create a larger, more complex view of ourselves—one that unlocks gates and opens up new pathways and, eventually, even new daydreams.

These repeated stories contain assumptions about yourself, other people, the world—assumptions that may hit you as "the truth," but which, as you see your feelings change, may slowly reveal themselves as old messages and may not seem as true to you now as they did in the past. Later we'll talk more about these assumptions and how to tease them out of your daydreams. But before we do, let's look closely at the thought chains associated with every daydream.

Jon's fantasies about Tracy were stimulated by seeing a woman who looked a little like her, hearing someone whose voice sounded like hers, doing something they used to do together. No surprises here. He imagined holding her, talking to her, making love to her. Still nothing new.

In fact, one reason Jon's daydreams were so repetitious was that it was hard for him to allow his thoughts to move randomly. These wandering thoughts are key to understanding your daydreams. To help Jon capture his, I suggested the following exercise. If you, too, are having difficulty allowing your thoughts to roam freely, you might want to try it as well.

EXERCISE:

FOLLOWING YOUR
THOUGHT CHAINS

1. Pull out your daydream diary and turn to a blank page.

2. Take a moment to look around you. Let your eyes drift. Make a mental note of some of the images you see. What attracts your attention? Does your eye fall on a favorite piece of furniture, a special picture, a hated vase or knickknack?

3. Close your eyes and try to focus on the first of those objects that comes into your mind. (If you simply can't focus, move on to the next step.)

4. Open your eyes, and at the top of the page write down the object you decided on in the last step. On the next line, write your next three thoughts. Don't take time to explore them. Don't worry if they don't make sense. And above all, don't try to organize them.

When Jon did this exercise, his eye fell on a red sweater that Tracy had often borrowed. Here is his list of associations:

Red—good color for her
Wish I could hold her
Should I try to get her back?

The last thought in this list indicated a story that was different from the ones we had been discussing. Anything new or different in a daydream association is always worth exploring, since it may indicate a window that you have just opened a crack, offering you a peek at a new aspect of the daydream's meaning. Each of these new twists will add to your store of clues and eventually lead to some of your personal organizing stories.

In Jon's case, the opening was onto another fantasy, one that he had not mentioned before. He said he sometimes thought about, even planned, various ways to get Tracy back. When I asked him if he could tell me more about these daydreams, he said he didn't like that I called them daydreams—he preferred to think of them as plans. I explained that I see plans as daydreams, since they are still in the world of the imagination, not action. Even if they seem completely realistic, they are stories that you tell yourself—stories that, in this case, were especially interesting because, however realistic they seemed to Jon, they contradicted his earlier conviction that he and Tracy could never reunite.

Jon's response—his next association—was also significant. "I guess I expected you to argue with me about fighting for Tracy. That was my next daydream." He grinned—he had obviously decided to play my "game," to refer to his inner scenarios as daydreams. He also seemed to take delight in the prospect of provoking me—getting me to fight with him. I asked him to put into words what the argument with me would be like—what I would say, what he would say in response. "You'd tell me to 'get real,' " Jon said, "to remember how awful it really was to live with Tracy, how we constantly carped at each other, how she kept putting me down, how I was always angry at her. I'd tell you that you didn't understand—that Tracy and I had a bond beneath all our fighting that made it worth the struggle." Jon's fantasy argument with me gained steam. "Then you'd say, 'But look at how she always tore you down, made you feel like a failure because you didn't have a better job.' And I'd say, 'Well, maybe Tracy was right to push me to something better—maybe she was just trying to get me off my duff and make something better of myself.' " In his imagination, Jon had created quite an animated fight between us—me arguing against Tracy, him arguing for her. I asked if any of the lines he'd given me were thoughts he had ever had. This is another useful question to ask yourself: sometimes we ascribe to someone else one side of an argument and we take another, in an attempt to resolve a conflict we are actually having within ourselves. It took Jon just a minute to remember that this argument with me wasn't really happening, except in his head. His answer went straight to the point: "You know something? As much as I hated Tracy for tearing me down all the time, I think some secret part of me was convinced she was right—that I *am* a screw-up. I mean, I *did* hate the fact that she was always riding me, but now I see that it was like she was telling me the truth about myself, even if I hated hearing it. I guess I was trying to provoke you into getting mad at me, too. I wanted you to tell the 'truth' about me, too. About me and Tracy. And I wanted to get mad at you for telling me the truth. I guess then I wouldn't have to face what I know."

Jon had opened quite a Pandora's box. As he talked more about the contradictory feelings contained in his obsession with Tracy, new understandings of himself emerged. Losing himself in "positive" daydreams about the physical sensations of making love to Tracy was, in part, his unconscious attempt to distract himself from some more painful truths, feelings he found it hard to tolerate. "The best thing about our life together was sex," Jon said, "and I guess I've fixated on that because it *was* the most positive thing. But more was going on. I see now that I stayed with Tracy because she was telling me something I know about myself—that I don't push myself, that I *could* be a lot better than I am—but as long as I heard from her, I could hate *her,* and not face myself. And as long as I thought about how much I missed her and loved her and wanted her back, as long as I thought about all the good things in our relationship, I still didn't have to deal with the other truth—that nobody else is going to pull my life together for me. If *I* don't do it, it won't get done."

As Jon paid more attention to his obsessive daydreams about Tracy, and as he followed the thoughts and feelings that slowly emerged in relation to his longing for her, he discovered he was dealing with a much more complex picture than he'd anticipated. But he also developed a stronger sense of what he was struggling with. He saw that he had a number of warring feelings, not only about Tracy, but also about himself.

UNKNOWN THOUGHTS

Daydreams almost always communicate—albeit obliquely—ideas that you believe but cannot necessarily name or describe. This illuminates the category of what the British author and psychoanalyst Christopher Bollas has called "the unthought known": that is, assumptions you make and ideas that you know but may never have noticed or even put into words. This "unthought known" material may be threaded through daydreams of physical sensations—sound, smell, touch. It may be hidden in visual dramas that are so familiar to you that you don't think to question them. Or, as Jon discovered, sometimes the simple *frequency* with which they hit you, the completeness with which they obsess you, can indicate the existence of feelings or thoughts that you are unconsciously striving to repress.

It's natural—at times even healthy—to keep certain information from ourselves, often the way we manage to get through the difficult process we call life. This is why we distort some of our thoughts or bury them in the symbolic meaning of our daydreams, and why the associative process I'm describing can be so hard. If we were comfortable with the information hidden in our daydreams, we would communicate it to ourselves in a far more direct way.

So what's the value of contemplating this frequently unpleasant and contradictory "unthought" material? The purpose is not to disturb you, although exploring it may indeed be disturbing at first. We do communicate it, although in disguised form. It is important information even when we're not ready to think directly about it or let ourselves feel the emotions connected to it. The more we can put these feelings into words, the more we know about them, the greater is our capacity to manage them and to integrate them into a fuller sense of ourselves.

Jon discovered that, as he started to recognize his ambivalent attitude not only toward Tracy but also toward himself, he had a clearer picture of *what he thought,* and a clearer insight into his assumptions about how he viewed himself and what he unconsciously expected (and as a result often found) in relationships with other people. When he realized that he was starting to see me as an angry, critical Tracy, he came face to face with the awareness that this was what he always anticipated—even looked for—in women.

The train of associations didn't stop here. At one point while he was daydreaming about Tracy, Jon found himself spontaneously thinking of his mother. He felt that she was always pushing him to improve himself, and he was always rebelling against her. I suggested that he ask himself some questions—questions you, too, can ask about patterns you begin to discover in your daydreams: Was he unconsciously *looking* for women to repeat this pattern? Was it just that it was comfortable to him, a familiar way of interacting? Could there possibly be something positive in this apparently negative pattern? "In a funny way, it lets me off the hook. I never have to face my own dissatisfaction. It's always the woman who is pointing out my failings," he told me.

His thoughts moved on to his friendships and to relationships at work, where he found the same theme repeated. "It's not just women who I see as criticizing me," he noted. "I do it with my boss, who's a man. I guess, when I see someone as an authority, I assume they're going to be critical of me. But I'm starting to see that some of that criticism is actually coming from me. I haven't been ready to look at my own conflicts about my behavior."

Even now that he was aware of these conflicts, Jon didn't always find it easy to think about them. It takes effort and time to recognize the confusing ideas and different aspects of ourselves that begin to become apparent when we look at our organizing stories. But putting some of his unspoken—and unknown—feelings into words eventually allowed Jon to gain some control over his obsession with Tracy—not all at once, but by degrees. Now that he was more conscious of the range of his feelings—not just love, but also resentment, anger, and an avoidance of his own responsibility—he could no longer "buy" the daydreams of "perfect happiness" with Tracy that had formerly obsessed him. The contradictory feelings that had fueled his obsession were given more direct expression, which meant the obsession began to lose its hold and purpose. Over time, he began to feel more whole, more complete, and *freer* as he struggled to think about a range of thoughts and images about Tracy—and about himself.

ASSOCIATING TO YOUR DAYDREAMS

Perhaps you are put off by—even a little uncomfortable with—the idea of associating to your daydreams. "Free association" is another of those fancy names for something you actually do every day: letting your mind wander. But whereas you probably automatically pull your mind back to whatever it is you're doing when it starts to roam, when you're analyzing your daydreams you will want to pay attention to these wanderings. This is another deceptively simple-sounding assignment. In fact, seasoned therapists, who learn to free-associate as part of their training, can still have difficulty with the process at times. So don't worry if you haven't quite "gotten it" yet. Every exercise and every example in this book will take you one step closer to being able to follow your wandering thoughts, and to using them to decode your daydream communications.

If, on the other hand, you're worried that you will become more obsessed, more stuck in your daydreams than you already are, just remember what Jon learned. A repeated daydream often indicates some internal communication that you are not hearing—perhaps not accepting. As you open up your internal lines of communication, these daydreams will lose their power. You will feel freer to move on—to make other choices in both your imaginary and your actual life.

However, as you come "unstuck," don't be surprised if you notice feelings that make you uncomfortable—that make you wonder why you're doing this at all. We weave our daydreams to cope with feelings and experiences that might otherwise overwhelm us, so taking them apart is bound to stir up some anxiety. But the very process of examining your daydreams is like a mental workout—a stretching and strengthening of the mental and emotional muscles you need to cope with the internal messages we're beginning to decipher. You'll see how this works even more clearly in the next chapters, where we'll talk about how daydreams can keep you tied to old beliefs and how they can help you cope with some of your worst fears.

CHAPTER THREE

Through the Looking Glass: Searching for the Familiar in the Unfamiliar

BARBARA, A PHOTOGRAPHER FRIEND of mine who lives in New York City, says she cannot understand how people can read while they're riding the buses and subways of Manhattan. To her the world of people in front of her is far more interesting than the stock prices in *The Wall Street Journal*.

"The *images* I see!" she rhapsodizes. "The stories on people's faces—the way they stand and move—there's just so much going on in the average rush-hour bus."

Once when we were on a subway together, she showed me just what she meant.

A young man with a knapsack got on the train and sat across from us. Barbara told me her daydream about him. "That young man is starting college next week—I assume from the T-shirt he's wearing that he's going to NYU. It's a big school, and he's nervous about getting lost in the crowd. But he's from a small town, and he's excited about being in New York City. He'll be in a relationship within a month." I must have looked doubtful—even in a daydream, how could she predict that? She answered my unasked question. "He needs a relationship to give him a sense of security in this exciting, frightening big city." She warmed to the subject. "But once he's in the relationship, he'll soon start to resent being tied down by it. He'll want his freedom. He won't recognize that he only wants freedom in the abstract—that he's anxious without a stabilizing person in his life."

Barbara, who knows me very well, grinned disarmingly. "I know, I know—these fantasies tell a lot more about me than they do about that guy." I nodded. Barbara needs no prodding to get to her daydream associations. Her fantasies and the connections she makes to them activate her creativity, so she's always paying attention to them.

Since she knows that I'm interested in this material, she happily shared some of her next thoughts. "When I saw him, he reminded me of myself when I came to New York—many years ago. I was excited and scared, in equal parts. I had never been on my own before, and I was thrilled about it, but also frightened. I got into a relationship right away. . . . Oh! That reminds me. Did you hear that Margo [a mutual friend of ours] is moving to Connecticut to be with her new love?" We talked for a few minutes about Margo and her move, and then Barbara went on: "You know, I guess I'd like to have some of that excitement in my life again. Maybe that's what I was seeing in that young man—my own wish to be excited and scared about something new. Margo's going to have that. I'm not interested in moving out of the city, or being tied down to a house, but . . ."

Barbara's fantasies about the people she sees play a crucial role in her photography. Her personal images come out in some way in every picture. But these daydreams are also useful information about what is going on inside of her—information that can be understood as she follows the threads of her thoughts through the tales she spins.

You may be saying to yourself, "It's easy for an artist to follow her daydream thoughts like that. I'm not creative. My daydreams are ordinary, just like the thoughts that come with them."

In fact, daydreams and creativity are spawned in the same place: what the child psychologist Charles Sarnoff calls our "active imagination." Barbara is able to follow her daydream thoughts because she has learned not to close down this part of her fantasy world. When you were a child, you probably had this capacity as well. You more than likely allowed your daydreams and the related thoughts and feelings to emerge without questioning or criticizing them. Playing in the backyard, you'd imagine that the fallen trunk of a tree was a pirate ship. You'd look up at the clouds and see a prince lovingly holding hands with a princess. You'd let your mind drift as you looked out the window on a rainy day and imagined that you were in a submarine, investigating all the strange sea life at the bottom of the ocean. . . .

Now, however, you may feel shy about pursuing such whimsical images. They may seem childish or silly, or you may still be convinced that they won't get you anywhere except "off the track" of whatever you're concentrating on. Or perhaps you're concerned that you simply can't do it—you might be able to let your mind wander freely (maybe), but you'll never come up with such fantastical notions, no matter how hard you try. Your stories are all about common, everyday things—whether you can let the kids skip their baths tonight, when you can squeeze a haircut (forget the manicure) into your schedule, what you're going to have for dinner.

By now you know that your daydream thoughts are far from silly or meaningless. You've seen that "off the track" is often right on target in daydream analysis; that apparently unrelated thoughts are frequently part of the unthought known that leads to self-awareness. But what can these fragmented, mundane thoughts of yours offer you? They are, first of all, your most accessible daydream thoughts, and therefore a path to other, less available daydreams and associations (remember Betty's daydream reminder to "buy milk"?); second, as you explore the stories they tell (and the stories they hide), you will strengthen your fantasy muscles, making it increasingly easier to find and investigate some of the unquestioned assumptions that inform your daily decisions and choices. That's where we're headed now—to examine your daydream stories for the beliefs they capture, convey, and perpetuate. Don't worry if you still don't think that you can "create" any interesting stories. They're already there, inside you, even if you don't have access to them yet; and as you read the examples and do the exercises in the next chapters, you will find them emerging—quietly, slowly, perhaps, but with results that will be both surprising and intriguing.

Bernie, a computer analyst, says he doesn't have an ounce of creativity in his body. He doesn't see that the very process of thinking about possible reasons for a computer problem is both original and inventive. When I pointed out that he is always generating ideas about probabilities that would never, ever occur to me (a computer illiterate), he was intrigued. "You mean I daydream about potential solutions," he said. He then went on to talk about cooking—a hobby that he loves but had never before thought of as particularly creative. "But I do the same thing when I cook. I read recipes, daydream about what they'll taste like and what other foods they would go with. . . . I can cook up a whole seven-course dinner in my imagination."

Why didn't Bernie see these thought processes as creative? Although the answer to this question (as to every question about our dynamics as human beings) is complex and multifaceted, it is in part related to some of the organizing stories that Bernie tells himself about who he is and how he lives his life.

"I was a brainy kid," he tells me," an egghead. I had friends, because I had a good sense of humor and I used it to my advantage. But deep down inside, I always knew I was a little 'off'—different from the other kids. I didn't play football or baseball, and I didn't go out with girls. But around exam time I always got very popular, because I was such a good student. I don't know what the kids expected—maybe that my ideas would just rub off on them, or maybe that I could convey my knowledge to them. But I've never been very good at teaching. I can know something and use that knowledge to do my work, but I can't always explain it to someone else.

"Maybe that's why I don't think of myself as creative. To this day I see myself as an awkward, clumsy adolescent who doesn't know what to do with his hands and hasn't got the slightest idea how to express himself."

Earlier I said that your daydreams contain un-thought-out assumptions about yourself, others, and the world—beliefs that color your attitudes and your behavior, affect your decisions, and alter your life. Bernie's image of himself as a perpetually awkward adolescent is what Dr. Daniel Stern, a psychiatrist who studies and writes about infant and child development, would call a "schema," meaning an ongoing representation of yourself in relation to other people that may occur to you as sensory impressions, or as daydreams you can't get away from, as they did with Jon. The scripts of your daydreams can be based on a combination of experiences. They can include some of your family's values and beliefs and your *perceptions* of those beliefs as a young child—personal stories that affect your behavior and color your experience every day. You take these familiar narratives into new situations, where you discover again what you already "know." Teasing out the themes of these stories will take you directly to some of the expectations that guide your life and give you a chance to decide just how valid they really are.

ORGANIZING STORIES

What exactly does an organizing story "look" like? How can you recognize your own—especially since they're usually something you've never really put into words or examined closely? Although it would be impossible to make a comprehensive list of all of the possible forms these scripts take, here's a brief summary of a few typical versions. Even if you don't find your own assumptions in this list, it will give you an idea of how they look and sound. Then the next example and the exercise that follows it will take you still closer to discovering these inner schemas that color your daydreams and organize your life.

I would be content if only I had . . . This is a common organizing story. Maybe you believe that, if you could only lose fifteen pounds, you would feel satisfied and happy. Or you may imagine that, if you had more money, more hair, better makeup, a more ambitious husband, or a sexy wife, you would never feel bad about yourself again. These are daydreams, of course, but they are also clues to organizing stories: assumptions about what it takes to be successful, satisfied with yourself, fulfilled. They are codes for some of your beliefs about the way the world works and the way you function in the world.

I am . . . Generalizations about yourself, whether positive or negative (or even neutral), are also keys to scripts you live by. These visions of ourselves are necessary: they make up our identities. But they can also create difficulties. If, like Bernie, you view yourself as the same person you were as a teenager or a child, you may expect people to respond to you as though you in fact still are that same person. Other people may not see you that way, but you can't take in this information. You're stuck in an outdated image of yourself, no matter what you really have become.

People are always . . . Any belief that people will consistently act or respond in a specific manner is a good clue to one of your basic assumptions. Although some of these generalizations will, of course, be based in reality, they will also often affect how you perceive and behave in any situation—at times perpetuating old beliefs and ruling out the possibility of new experiences with different people.

Like many of us, Patricia simply took as fact an organizing story that was actually an old family belief. She had never put this narrative into words, and she had therefore never opened it up for questioning. She had no idea that it was a family fantasy, or myth, that had become part of the way she lived her life.

Patricia grew up in a close-knit and self-contained family in which outsiders were seldom invited to share a meal. The family all agreed: "Other people are intruders." Patricia never thought about it. In fact, she assumed that *everyone* felt you couldn't trust anyone but "family." When her friends occasionally invited Patricia to dinner or to spend the night, she always felt uncomfortable, because she assumed they disliked having company as much as her own family did. It never occurred to her that some people might actually enjoy socializing.

Patricia was painfully shy, often experiencing herself as an intruder in somebody's else's space, always trying to make herself as small and inconspicuous as possible. When she came to see me, she was struggling with feelings of inadequacy and incompetence.

In some of her daydreams she was socially capable and assertive, but in real life she was always quiet and unassuming.

I asked about those "assertive" daydreams. "Sometimes I imagine walking up to people in the college cafeteria and introducing myself, asking if I could join them," Patricia said. "I imagine myself doing this—but I can never actually bring it off."

I asked what she imagined would happen if she tried.

"They'd be polite," she said, "but cold. They'd keep talking to each other and wouldn't include me. I'd feel like an idiot."

How did she explain this behavior? "Well, people don't like outsiders. That's just a fact." We were in familiar territory: Patricia had told me a great deal about her closed-off family, and she was aware that the family mistrust of "outsiders" hobbled her ability to connect with people in her life today. But she had never really questioned the truth of this belief—even while she recognized the negative effect that "truth" had on her life. For most of her life, it was beyond her comprehension that anyone could feel differently. "When I see someone at a party, telling jokes and talking easily to people, I always just assume it's an act—that they're *pretending* to be close and easy and open. I've always thought that to be 'social' you had to learn to pretend in this way, and that some people were just better at it than others. It never occurred to me that some people might genuinely *be* open and trusting."

What turned the tide for Patricia was her decision to act on her recurring assertive daydreams: to see what might happen if she actually did walk up to somebody and start a conversation. "The idea of actually doing it was terrifying to me," Patricia said, "but the more I realized that my fear of doing it was based on one story, and wasn't the only 'truth,' the more determined I was to carry it out. But I played it safe. I had noticed another quiet young woman in my English class at college, how she always seemed to keep to herself. One day I saw her in the cafeteria and drummed up my nerve—and walked over to her, asking her what she'd thought about class that day. It was incredible—she just seemed so happy that I'd come up to speak to her! She didn't react in any of the ways I'd feared. She wasn't cold at all. I guess some instinct must have told me she'd be safe to talk to, but I never anticipated how warm and open she would be. It jarred me—made me think that maybe you *didn't* have to navigate your way through the world as if everyone was in their own armed camps. . . ."

Patricia's assertive daydreams are less oblique than Jon's or Michael's, but they are no less packed with information about unsuspected feelings and beliefs. Perhaps the most surprising consequences of exploring those daydreams—along with her decision to act on the scenario she had played for herself so often in her imagination—was the powerful realization that her old, separatist assumptions weren't some immutable truth. They were tied to other, unquestioned beliefs that the world was "unsafe," but as she began to accept that these *were* assumptions, she felt more and more capable of entertaining new, more productive hypotheses about the world, other people, and, in turn, herself. "It's not going to happen overnight," Patricia said, "but proving to myself that I *can* after all connect with another human being really cracked my little self-contained egg. The world just might be wider and more welcoming than I'd ever thought." For Patricia, these daydreams actually served as *rehearsals* of what it might be like to reach out to someone else. They were sufficiently rooted in reality so that she could try them out—with some illuminating results.

How do you start to open up your own assumptions? It's not always easy, because, obviously, if you believe something is true, you're not going to question it. But the very fact that you now know that these stories exist will help you begin the process. Here are some more examples to help you think about your personal scripts. As you look them over, remember that we all have several stories by which we organize our experiences, and that they are by definition not always easy to tease out. Don't worry if you can't figure yours out right away. Simply looking for them will open a few interesting doors.

MORE ORGANIZING STORIES

"Other people are always smarter (happier, friendlier, more emotional, more connected, more assertive, etc.) than I am. That explains why I can't make friends (or find a job or stay in a relationship, etc.)."

"Other people are always less intelligent (less content, less friendly, less emotional, less connected, etc.) than I am. That explains why I can't find anyone I really like being with (or a job I like, etc.)."

"No one really understands me."

"I would never do to other people what they do to me. People are always picking on me, putting me down, dumping all their shit on me. It doesn't make any sense."

Organizing stories are often represented by short phrases or questions. When you try to explain the comments—with a line beginning "because" or "therefore"—or to answer the questions, you will discover more of the details of your stories. For example, you might routinely say to yourself, "I come from a crazy family." You explain, "therefore I can't possibly ever be happy." That's an organizing story.

One young woman I know frequently tells me that she would never dress in really form-fitting clothes. When I asked her to try to explain, she replied, "because men would come on to me and women would hate me." These sentences made up the tip of an iceberg of personal scripts about men who would not accept "no" for an answer and women who would tear her to shreds out of envy.

A man complains that everyone takes advantage of him. When he follows the sentence with "because," he is faced with his organizing story that he is such a wimp that no one respects him.

Many of us have organizing stories about our families. We sometimes use these scripts to explain, and sometimes we try to explain them with other thoughts. Here are just a few examples:

"Because I come from a perfect family I . . ."

"I come from a completely wretched, nonfunctional family, therefore I . . ."

"My family was (or was not) . . ."

"My mother (or father) did (or did not) . . . , therefore . . ."

"My husband (or wife, lover, roommate, boss, etc.) makes me . . ."

"I can never live up to my parents' expectations of me . . ."

"I can never be as good as my parents . . ."

"If I do well in life, my mother (or father) will feel like a success (or failure) . . ."

In our organizing stories we tell ourselves about our families of origin and our current family groups, our personal histories, our remembered past and our imagined future. Through them we place ourselves in our culture and our society. In other words, we use them for just what the phrase says: to organize our experience of ourselves and the world in which we live. Phrases like the ones above that capture any ongoing belief or attitude can be keys to your personal organizing stories. The next exercise will take you another step into *your* personal stories.

DISCOVERING THE HIDDEN ASSUMPTIONS IN YOUR DAYDREAMS

1. Take a moment to think back over your day so far. Focus on some moment that seemed problematic, some incident that left you feeling a little bit unhappy, frustrated, or dissatisfied. Don't look for a *big* issue, just a small snag in the course of your day. It can be something as simple as spilling the coffee grounds as you started to make your morning coffee. Go over that episode in your mind. Draw a mental picture of what happened and how you felt about it.

2. Now ask yourself this key question: how do you explain what happened? For example, do you say to yourself that you spilled the coffee because you're clumsy and uncoordinated? Or because you never pay attention to what you're doing? Or is it that you're trying to do too many things, and something always gets messed up? Or do you believe that *everybody* has difficulties in the morning and it doesn't mean anything?

As you answer these questions, look for tip-offs to some of the organizing stories you tell yourself—unspoken assumptions about who you are and how you function in the world. This may seem simple, but these answers are keys to more complex images that reinforce your feelings (both positive and negative) about yourself and the world in which you live. Dr. Catherine Steiner-Adair, a psychologist and therapist based in Boston and director of education, prevention, and outreach at the Harvard Eating Disorder Center, conducted some fascinating research about the psychological development of adolescent girls, exploring connections between organizing stories, body image, and self-esteem. She found that women who bought into cultural myths about beauty and personal perfection assumed that models' bodies were the "true" image of perfect femininity. These women were far less self-confident and far more focused on "fixing" their bodies than those whose personal stories included a genuine belief that they could—and should—feel good about themselves without looking like Madison Avenue's image of womanhood.

Do this exercise several times over the next few days. Don't be surprised if you find a number of different, possibly conflicting narratives. But each time you capture one, ask yourself one more question: what would happen if you didn't believe in this "truth"? Your answers will tell you something about your own fears; they may also lead to new daydreams, which can lead you, as they did Patricia, to new interactions and experiences in the world.

A WORD ABOUT "PARENT-BLAMING"

In recent years we have come to understand that parents have a crucial role in the psychological development of their children. Yet an unfortunate side-effect of this important knowledge is the tendency to explain all of our psychological makeup as the result of our parents' behavior and flaws. I would very much like to avoid that pitfall in this book, while at the same time recognizing that some of our conflicts do originate in our childhood experiences and the ways we explain those experiences to ourselves. As you will see in chapter 8, stories in which parents are seen only as angels or monsters can trap us in a one-dimensional view not only of them but also of ourselves and other people. We are all—parents included—mixtures of many different qualities. Opening up some of your images of important family members will enrich your perspective and expand your choices.

Once you start to notice some of the familiar tales in your daydreams, stories that you have told yourself for many years, pay special attention to the *complexity* of the pictures you are developing. Keep your eyes open for material you have never noticed before. As Patricia began to question her assumption that her parents were right that everyone disliked outsiders, she also began to wonder about other unquestioned beliefs she had held on to from childhood. For example, she had always thought of her parents as extremely strong, but now she wondered if their feelings about intrusion and strangers weren't actually based in extreme shyness and vulnerability to others. "They were trying—in their own way—to protect us kids from being hurt by other people. Unfortunately, it didn't work very well for me. I always felt hurt, because—although I didn't know it—I *wanted* those connections with others." But then she had another thought, one that brought more complexity into her picture of her parents: "Somehow they also helped me grow up stronger than them, able to tolerate whatever rejections I may get in life, in order to be close to people."

Gustave Flaubert once wrote, "To express what one wishes, one must look at things with enough attention to discover in them what has never been seen before." Once they had discovered some of the assumptions they operated on without realizing it, both Patricia and Jon could disagree with their family myths, while also understanding something about why their parents were the way they were. This ability to see our parents as human beings, and ourselves as adults in an equal relationship with them, is powerfully liberating. Jon, for example, told me that, as he thought about the stories in his daydreams, he began to talk more openly about some of these issues with his parents. "I had a conversation with my mother where I didn't feel like rebelling against everything she said. It was funny. She started her usual nudging, and I said, 'You're right. I really should do that.' She kept going, so I said it again. I guess she has assumptions about me, just like I do about her. When I had that thought, I was able to joke with her about how she wasn't listening to what I said. She laughed, and said something—I don't even remember what it was. But the tone in her voice was very loving. It reminded me of how close we were when I was a kid. And then I realized that I'd been thinking that she didn't love me. As a kid, I equated love with acceptance. But I think now that her love for me is actually *why* she's so critical. I don't like her way of expressing it. And I know I'm never going to get her to admit that she loves me despite my failings. I guess it's time to give up on the hope that she—or some woman who substitutes for her—is going to tell me how wonderful I am even though I've never gotten anywhere in my life." It took time, but this realization eventually freed Jon to start to figure out where *he* wanted to go with his life—for the first time in his life.

MORE ABOUT YOUR ORGANIZING STORIES

Your stories come from many places—not only childhood, family, and societal myths, but also from who you are now, what you do for a living, how you go through your life. The form and content of these inner tales are affected by everyone in your life—your lover, your children, your friends, your co-workers, the woman or man you see (but may not talk to) every day on the elevator or at the gym. Some of your personal stories may be based on books, television, the movies, the newspaper. They are often grounded in the culture in which you grew up, and the culture you live in now. But they are always specifically yours, and frequently come from a need to see the familiar in the unfamiliar, as well as from a wish to protect yourself from knowledge and feelings that might hurt you or leave you feeling unsafe or confused.

We all tell ourselves many different, even contradictory stories. This multiplicity of stories may be embedded in or hidden by the one recurring or even obsessive daydream you can't seem to get out of your head. Exploring your daydreams means opening yourself to the random thoughts that occur to you—and then asking yourself about the themes that tie these thoughts together. These associations will lead you to some of your other stories and will eventually provide the keys to your daydream symbols.

Sometimes, as with Patricia, a daydream can act as a sort of "rehearsal": a way in which you try out a new activity in your imagination. Sometimes—even at the same time—daydreams are much more complex condensations of feelings and thoughts you'd rather not face head-on, coupled with more pleasant fantasies that give outward form to the daydream. As you gather information about yourself, you will learn ever more clearly that there is no such thing as a single truth: reality is a complex tangle of threads woven from numerous stories we tell ourselves.

We've begun to tease out the mysterious web of meaning that daydreams offer us. Now it's time to focus in a bit more squarely on the "forbidden" messages daydreams often encode. One of the important functions of daydreams, as we've seen, is to codify feelings and thoughts that disturb us—that would threaten us if we apprehended them in more direct form. This function— of processing troubling feelings and turning them into something tolerable, manageable—is one of the essential gifts our daydreams give us. But as you'll see in the next chapter, we process not only our own feelings in daydreams—they are sometimes a means of making internal sense of other people's feelings as well. In fact, daydreams sometimes represent thoughts we don't even know we're having about what's going on inside someone else.

Let's find out more about this protective and communicative function of daydreams, and how to discover and explore what secret feelings they are communicating to us—our own unexpressed feelings and those we sense from others around us.

CHAPTER FOUR

Embroidering Beasts: Using Daydreams to Cope with Fears—Yours and Other People's

IN ISABEL ALLENDE'S magical—and horrifying—novel *The House of Spirits*, Rosa, the eldest daughter in her family, uses her daydreams to escape temporarily from frightening undercurrents that eventually destroy other members of the household. Allende describes her as "dreaming of new beasts to embroider on her tablecloth, creatures that were half-bird and half-mammal, covered with iridescent feathers and endowed with horns and hooves, and so fat and with such shabby wings that they defied the laws of biology and aerodynamics." Rosa's daydreams actually hint at horrors to come in her own family, terrors created by human beasts, from which the family members discover that their own "shabby wings" render them unable to fly. But initially the images of these daydreams are presented to us (the reader), and are also apparently experienced by Rosa, in such a benign manner that we do not yet sense the impending disasters. Rosa's daydream is beautiful, if a little bizarre: the beauty of the daydream protects her from presentiments of doom she does not consciously want to face. Even so, those presentiments—and the fears that are bound up in them—are "embroidered" into the daydream. As the story unfolds and we learn more about Rosa and her world, we gradually come to understand, even to experience, what these creatures represented for her.

Allende's mystical images and powerful use of language offer a perfect illustration of how daydream codes combine verbal and nonverbal symbols—and can sometimes mask frightening fears and feelings, making them more consciously tolerable. The vivid visual images (although of course conveyed to us in the novel via language) of "half-bird" and "half-mammal" show us a kind of horrible hybrid beast; and yet the beauty and control of the language in which those images are portrayed *calms* the effect of this alarming vision: we are distracted by the "iridescent" feathers from the unpleasant image of fat and sagging wings that would seem to make it impossible for these beasts to fly. . . .

In our daydreams we often condense disturbing feelings into images that distract us from ideas we are not ready to face more directly. Allende uses Rosa's daydream beasts to convey something about the repressed violence that was soon to break loose from its constraints, although the reader only comes to this realization as the book unfolds. This literary device parallels our work with daydreams in two ways. Like Rosa's beasts, daydream imagery can serve as a metaphor through which we simultaneously conceal and indirectly reveal unrecognized information; and the interpretation of these symbols can only occur after we have allowed not just the images but also many subsequent thoughts to unfold and play themselves out.

FROM FEELINGS TO WORDS

Symbols can be obscure, but we make use of them all the time—and not only in daydreams. According to Dr. Charles Sarnoff, the child psychiatrist who wrote about "active imagination," we begin using symbols to think before we are eight months old. When we start to talk, we immediately begin to use language to help us organize and think about what we know, and to communicate that knowledge to others. The use of symbolic language allows our thinking to become more sophisticated and complex. We use it to capture and classify some of the subtle nuances of events, feelings, and thoughts that we encounter in ourselves and others. But some thoughts and feelings cannot be put into words. They feel dangerous—unmanageable—and we keep them in the realm of nonverbal metaphor and imagery. These two sets of symbols—verbal and nonverbal—often work together to disguise and distort the information daydreams offer you.

Dr. Virginia Demos, a psychologist who studies and works with infants and children, has focused on the ways we use language to codify feelings. She has found that many of us are afraid to put certain feelings into words precisely because naming them makes them more visible to us and therefore, we believe, more painful. Subconsciously, we hope that we can avoid whatever unpleasantness the feelings will bring us by not naming them. We've already explored this self-protective impulse to some degree, particularly in Michael's daydreams of Paris, and Jon's daydreams about Tracy. These unverbalized feelings continue to affect us even though we have kept them in the realm of the unnamed. Paradoxically, putting your daydreams into words sometimes actually helps make these unarticulated dangers less frightening.

Just as Rosa's daydream of embroidering beasts was a way she told herself (and didn't let herself know) about some of the things she thought and felt about her own family, so, too, your own daydreams can be psychic attempts to express to yourself your emotional responses to the people around you.

As a psychotherapist, I frequently find that my own daydreams are signals for unformed ideas about clients and their situations that are beginning to emerge from my subconscious. Since these daydreams never come to me all at once, I have learned to wait and watch and listen—allowing them to unfold in their own time and space. Eventually, over time, as I follow the steps I suggested to you in chapter 2, my daydreams begin to crystallize into some very useful ideas. Why I can't just "get it" all at once—tell myself directly what I'm sensing—isn't always clear. Sometimes it has to do with my personality (my own unconscious blocks about what I'd rather hear and not hear), sometimes with the way a particular story is unfolding (it may be more than usually oblique or disorganized). These daydreams, and the associations I make to them, are extremely helpful ways for me to gain access to unspoken (even to myself), otherwise inaccessible ideas about information I'm gathering from other people.

Your own daydreams often help you to process information about other people in similar ways: they can be a way of symbolically communicating what you think about *others* as well as about yourself. This happened vividly for me a number of years ago in a women's group I had been working with for quite a while. One night, while two members of the group were talking about difficulties they'd been having with their respective lovers, I began to think about a child swimming in the ocean. I couldn't figure out what that image had to do with what the women were talking about—it seemed to come out of nowhere. But I knew my own thought processes well enough to believe that, if I let the image develop over time, I would very likely learn something significant about both myself and the group members. The picture of that child in the ocean often recurred for me, new details emerging at every session. After each group meeting, I would take a little time to write down these new developments in the story, and then, for about five minutes, I would make brief notes on *any* thoughts that occurred to me. Some of my associations seemed dull and uninteresting, and others appeared wildly off the mark, but I kept at it until, eventually, I began to see what I was telling myself. It was such a powerful communication that I shared it with the group. Here's how the daydream story emerged:

I imagine a little girl, just beginning to walk, at the beach with her family. When they get to the ocean, her mother takes one of her hands and her father the other, and they wade out into the water. The baby giggles as the water laps at her chubby legs, and chortles with glee as her parents "jump" her over the little waves breaking at her feet. They let go of her hands, and she sits happily in the water until a sudden wave hits her in the face. Her parents quickly pick her up, make sure she is all right, cuddle and soothe her until she is comforted.

In some of my daydreams, the little girl demands to sit back down in the water; in others, she is too frightened, and her parents hold her by the hands again, lift her over the tiny waves, and wait till she feels safe and secure enough to play in the water again.

Then my mind rolls the clock forward. It is the next year, and the little girl is back at the beach, but now, although she is physically larger and stronger and more sure on her feet, she is a little frightened of the water. She has learned that the world is not always comfortable and safe, and she is not so sure she wants to move out into these very visibly active seas.

One time her father takes her in his arms and wades out beyond the breakers. The little girl clings tightly, but she trusts that her parents can manage the waves even though she cannot. She enjoys this experience, and now she decides to try to ride the waves on her own. She slips out of her father's arms before he knows what's happening and sinks down in the water. Her parents pick her up before any serious harm has been done, but she is miserable, coughing, crying, and saying she wants to go home.

It is a little more difficult for the parents to soothe her this time. They do not want her to be overly frightened of the water, but they recognize that it is important for her to have a healthy respect for its power and the potential danger of going in beyond her own level of competence.

That winter, the child takes swimming lessons. She grows taller and stronger and more physically capable, and when she gets to the ocean the next summer, she is more competent and confident in the water. Though she does not swim without an adult watching her, she now she happily rides the waves and plays in the water. Even when she is knocked over by a wave, when she scrapes her stomach on the sand and swallows too much salt water, she comes up spluttering and screaming, but not in terror.

My daydream continued to spin out. I saw the girl grow into a young woman, a strong swimmer who no longer needs her parents with her to deal with the waves and currents of the ocean. I imagined that she has learned it is always a good idea to have another person with her when she goes out swimming, just in case something comes up that she cannot handle alone. She knows this is a sign not of weakness but of strength. She can handle the waves on her own, but the presence of another person enhances her capacity to function in any given situation.

The story did not come out in a whole piece like this for quite a while. In the meantime, I had many associations—memories, images, feelings, and thoughts—some of which were about my own childhood family vacations at the North Carolina beaches. I remembered times when I was tossed around by the ocean. Images of rainy days when I missed my friends back home, or when I felt cozy and happy with my family, melded with memories of long days spent sunbathing and reading on the beach. As I let myself wander through the daydream associations, the images shifted to my early teens vacationing at the same beach, where my growing interest in boys, developing sexuality, and terrible vulnerability about peer approval made my life absolutely miserable. But as I put my associations together, I realized that the beach of my daydreams did not simply represent my own personal development. The ocean and waves symbolized feelings; and learning to swim was my image for learning to deal with the turmoil and waves of feelings that we all struggle to cope with throughout life.

Because I thought the daydream captured something that the members of the group were grappling with, I shared it with them—with astonishing results. Each member of the group had a very vivid and immediate personal image to add to the story—this story about dealing with feelings, learning, so to speak, to "ride the waves." The images each of them came up with told something important about the way that particular woman was struggling to cope with the waves of her feelings as an adult.

Terry spoke of a memory of pretending that she could swim, although she couldn't, and nearly drowning as a result. In the group and in her life, because Terry had difficulty admitting that she was vulnerable and that she ever needed help from anyone else, she often got herself into impossible situations. We had never been able to put this into words so clearly before

Elissa spoke of being a strong swimmer but afraid of the ocean, "because you never know when there might be a current

that would pull you under or wash you out to sea." Elissa, a successful professional, was frightened of being hurt in her personal
life, and therefore was having difficulties making a commitment in
a love relationship. The image made her fear more poignant and
more understandable. As she associated to it over time, she realized it captured her anxiety that she would be sucked up into
other people if she allowed herself to become even slightly dependent on them. As she put it, "I'm afraid I'll lose my *self,* my identity—maybe even my existence—if I become dependent on
someone else."

The point here was that my developing daydream was a
story filled with information about my own dynamics and the
"currents" I was sensing from each woman in the group: the
image of a girl learning to swim in the ocean, dealing with her
fears, growing in competence, had occurred to me because, on
both a narrative and a symbolic level, it was what each of the
women in my group was telling me concerned her most. It is significant that my daydream was, in fact, *mine:* it had deep and
immediate meaning to me and arose from my own feelings and
experience. But it was also my psyche's attempt (successful, it
turns out) to tell me what I was hearing from the rest of the
women in the group. The daydream helped to *connect* all of us—
not merely to express something idiosyncratic and unshareable
from each particular one of us. It also captured something of the
healing, supportive function of the group itself, which enhanced
the members' capacity to face these difficult feelings.

Like Isabel Allende's Rosa, by drawing on my own pool of
conscious and unconscious symbols, I constructed an image that
made sense of the currents I perceived in the people in the group.
This image—put into words—represented my unrecognized
thoughts in the most vivid and apt way possible. The words then
made it possible for us—the group members and me—to make
contact with feelings that had previously been unavailable to us.
The ocean represented painful emotions that the women in the

group had been talking "around" without talking "about." Interestingly, once we connected with the feelings that this image of the ocean engendered in us, we could in fact discuss other difficult issues more openly and easily. We made contact with these sentiments through the imagery of the daydream—which opened the door to more particular and delicate personal explorations that each now found it more tolerable to pursue.

DAYDREAMS DEALING WITH GRIEF

Just as the image of the girl swimming in the ocean opened up my group's and my own ability to explore some very vulnerable territory in ourselves, Ellie, a single mother whose own mother had become terminally ill with cancer, found a daydream image—one that would prove to have profound meaning—in snow. After attending a daydream workshop that I ran, Ellie told me the following fantasy:

"I was taking a long walk. It was a beautiful winter day. There was fresh, new-fallen snow on the ground, sparkling white in the sun. It was cold, but not uncomfortable. I took a deep breath of the clean air. I knew my mother was dead—that she had died some time ago. In the daydream, I had already finished grieving, and now I was ready to live—to start my own life again."

Ellie thought the daydream was crystal-clear: "I don't want to grieve. I want to have it over with. But," she went on, "I realized after thinking about that daydream that that's not the way it works. I have to grieve. I'm starting to see that all this anger that I've been feeling—I've been sniping at my kids lately, and I seem to have no patience for any frustration—is my way of avoiding the sadness and the pain. I guess in my daydream I was trying to get it over with, but I was also telling myself that I have to feel the sadness before I can move on and start my own life again."

Ellie translated the visual images of a clear winter day and new-fallen snow, and the physical sensation of taking a deep breath of clear, fresh air, into feelings—a sense of relief and a feeling of "starting afresh." Then she could look at the most obvious meaning of the daydream, which was that she wanted her mother to go ahead and die. Although it was painful to recognize even this meaning, Ellie knew it made sense. She hated to see her mother suffer, she knew death was going to come anyway, and she was under tremendous pressure while her mother was ill (she was her mother's primary caretaker in addition to keeping her own kids and household going). By letting herself recognize and accept it, by not criticizing herself for having these (very normal) feelings, Ellie also opened herself up to understanding a second, less obvious meaning of her daydream—that she wasn't letting herself feel the pain of the losses she was experiencing.

It wasn't just that her mother was dying, but also that, as a result of the illness, Ellie had lost her mother as a support, as a helper, as a confidante. Even though her mother had not literally taken care of her for many years, she had often pitched in to help with the children when Ellie needed her, and she had always been there emotionally for Ellie. So her mother's illness was the cause of both emotional and concrete losses for Ellie. And it was a fore-runner of the loss that was to come—the loss of her mother's pres-ence altogether. The daydream captured not only Ellie's readiness to grapple with (and gradually to accept) her mother's potential death, but also her conflicting wish to "freeze" these feelings and not feel them.

Just as my group members and I discovered, Ellie found that putting previously unexpressed feelings into words actually made them more tolerable. Eventually, having verbalized the feelings, you can find ways other than your usual ones (whatever those may be) to cope with them; and you can gradually move on from them. In the process, you discover that feelings aren't static. Ellie became more tolerant of and even sympathetic with herself when she realized that she had a whole welter of constantly shifting emotions: sorrow, anger, fear, impatience, a desire for peace—both for her mother and for herself. Her lesson wasn't simply that she needed to grieve, but that she was struggling with a rich brew of feelings, that she felt a lot more than she'd realized. Putting these emotions into words gave her a new internal connection to herself, and strengthened her capacity to cope with the difficult time in her life. This widened her self-view—showing that she was a more complex person with more emotional resources than she'd given herself credit for.

There was (as there always is) still more to Ellie's daydream. Like my image of the child in the sea, her image of fresh snow captured not just her own unthought feelings, but also her reactions to unarticulated emotions communicated by the people around her—in this case, her mother and children. "None of us is ready to deal with this," she told me. "I heard my daughter crying in her room last night. My first impulse was to walk right by. I thought I couldn't possibly bear her pain as well as mine. But I remembered my image of that cold, fresh air, took a deep breath, and went into her room. We talked for a long time about all sorts of things: Mom, and death, and what would happen to the kids if I died. We held on to each other and cried—and it wasn't nearly as bad as I thought it was going to be. I wonder if I should try to talk to my mom. . . . I'm afraid of seeing her cry . . . but I know she's been wanting to talk about it. Every time she brings it up, I say, 'You're going to live forever, Mom.' Maybe I'm not being fair to her. And maybe it would even make me feel better—a relief, at least, just like talking about my own feelings has been."

The image of snow in Ellie's daydream could, of course, have been interpreted in other ways. But Ellie felt quite clear: for her, the snow and the crisp, cold air opened the way to feelings—her own and other people's—that she had not allowed herself to recognize before.

CONNECTING VERBAL AND NONVERBAL SYMBOLS

Though the focus of this chapter has been on exploring daydreams as a means of apprehending unrecognized feelings—both yours and those of others around you—in fact (as you've discovered already if you've done the earlier exercises in this book) *anything and everything* can come up in your daydreams. Every exercise in this book is geared to helping you get out of the way of the flow of your own thoughts and feelings. The next exercise will help you to gain a better, more visceral understanding of just how images and other sensory impressions can wed with language to produce some extraordinary condensed messages in daydreams—as extraordinary as Allende's embroidery of beasts.

EXERCISE:

NAME THAT FEELING

You will need your daydream diary, a pen, and your favorite magazine (glue and scissors are optional).

1. Take out your daydream diary, but don't open it up yet.

2. Flip through the pages of your magazine until you come to a picture that interests you. Don't concentrate on this part of the exercise: let your eyes and mind drift until something grabs your attention.

3. On a blank page of your daydream diary, briefly describe the picture; or, if you prefer, you can cut it out and glue it into your book. Make sure there are several blank lines beneath the description or picture.

4. On these blank lines, write four or five words about the image. Don't stop to think about them, and don't organize your

thoughts or censor yourself. Just write the first words that come to your mind.

For example, Deborah, who was trying to get pregnant and could think of almost nothing else, clipped out a picture of a pregnant woman and an advertisement for baby equipment. The words she wrote included: "love," "special," "cuddling," "happy," "ache," and "sad."

5. Look at the words you've written. Pay special attention to the words that express some emotion. As you're starting to see, some of the most powerful clues to the meanings of daydreams lie in the feelings that are either expressed by or hidden in them.

6. Notice what other words, stories, or images come to your mind when you think about these words?

Deborah wanted to be pregnant, to have a child growing inside her, a baby to love and cuddle. She imagined feeling special to that baby: "After all," she often said, "who is more special than your mother?"

But what about the other words: "ache" and "sad"? Deborah was worried that she would not be able to have the baby she wanted so desperately. Although she had only begun trying to start a family a month before she did this exercise, she told herself that she should not get her hopes up—that she was likely to be disappointed. This thought connected with many past experiences. It was not, for Deborah, specifically a feeling she had about having a baby, but a narrative that colored most of her experience. She *planned* for disappointment, expected it. Indeed, one of her organizing stories—the way she organized much of her life—was the following assumption: "The one thing you can count on in life is that you will be disappointed."

Deborah tried to protect herself from disappointment by preparing for it—in a sense, rehearsing how she would feel when it inevitably came. At least she would not let herself be taken by surprise.

There was another story in Deborah's daydreams as well, this one about the way she imagined herself as a mother. Next to a magazine picture of a mother and baby she wrote the words "good" and "caring." Just what she meant became clear as she talked about her associations: "I'll be a good and caring mother. I'll *want* to do things for my baby." Deborah had always worried about being "too selfish and self-centered." She was extremely critical of these qualities, in other people as well as herself. This was an aspect of herself that she disliked intensely.

In her daydreams of what it would be like to be a mother, Deborah imagined a different self. She would be the opposite of selfish: she would be caring, giving, make herself completely available to her baby. I asked her to tell me the first thoughts that came to her mind when she heard the words "good" and "caring" and "unselfish." "A perfect mother," was her automatic response. Desperately afraid of being less than "selfless," Deborah drummed into herself a sort of pledge to be that perfectly caring mother—as if a perfectly good mother could have no other (less acceptable) feelings.

Deborah's associations reveal (at times by expressing the opposite of) some of her most urgent fears. Sometimes we use daydreams (both consciously and unconsciously) as a kind of talisman against disaster—either by preparing ourselves for it (Deborah's assumption that she'd be disappointed) or by assiduously clinging to "good" outcomes—seeing ourselves as the perfect people we think we have to be. What Deborah began to see was that she was afraid that just being herself would not be good enough—she could not be the mother she dreamed of being.

Don't expect your own hidden fears just to pop out as you associate to the pictures you've chosen. It will be useful to do this exercise more than once. Think of it as you do a workout at the gym: repeating it over time will build strength and skill. Each time you do it, pay attention to the words and phrases that you come up with. Then ask yourself what stories go with these feelings, and why you think these stories are coming up now.

These are not simple or easy questions to answer. But each time you ask them, you are building more muscles for feeling and fantasy. As you go along, you will find that putting your stories into words will gradually strengthen your ability to open up unrecognized—and highly meaningful—internal communications and sort out and discard old, unhelpful assumptions. Gradually you will develop more complex and useful images of yourself and the important people in your life.

CHAPTER FIVE

The Moon Reflects the Sun: How Daydreams and Night Dreams Connect

NOW THAT YOU'VE BEGUN to explore your daydreams, it's likely you've been thinking more about your night dreams, too. Is there a connection between them?

Certainly most people feel their night dreams are more exotic, strange, and interesting than their daydreams, which, as we've seen, can be as ordinary as musing about the milk, paper towels, and eggs you have to pick up tonight at the supermarket.

Night dreams are usually packed with images, filled with symbols, markers that seem to indicate deep unconscious meanings. Daydreams, by contrast, can seem awfully commonplace. But by now you know this is a misperception—a misunderstanding of what is really going on in your daydreams.

The dreams we dream when asleep have long tantalized human beings. Ancient people thought their night dreams contained messages from the gods. Special people were chosen to interpret the meaning of these communications—Joseph, for example, in the Old Testament translated the pharaoh's dreams to prophesy the upcoming years of feast and famine; the oracle of Delphi in ancient Greece explained the dream that foretold that Oedipus would kill his father and marry his mother. More recently, Freud maintained that dreams hold the keys to self-knowledge. Jung based a whole psychology on the interpretation of dreams and the archetypes he believed were to be found in them. Numerous psychological theorists have since added to a burgeoning literature on night dreams—continuing a tradition of dream-deciphering that probably began when the first human beings woke up in a cave and wondered about the strange, dark images that had so haunted them during the night.

But contemporary research is revealing that night dreams may be a good deal less mysterious than mystics and many psychoanalysts would have us believe. Dr. Harry Fiss is a psychologist who studies dreams at the University of Connecticut. He says that the baffling images and stories in night dreams are the result of neurological and physiological changes that occur when we sleep. Because of these alterations in our physical makeup, we actually think differently when we're asleep and when we're awake. And these differences make the symbols of our night dreams much less logical and clear-cut, much more vivid and outlandish than those of our daydreams. Arguably, so many of your daydreams seem comparatively coherent and commonplace because your waking thought processes simply *are* more coherent and better organized than your sleeping ones.

But this doesn't change the fact that your dreams—day or night—are chock-full of meaning. Both types of dream contain indirect communications in the form of symbols and code; even if neurological and physiological changes in the body and brain may be adding an extra spice to those symbols, your mind is still frequently trying to tell you something—and often, as we'll see in this chapter and the rest of the book, wrestling with dilemmas and challenges it wants to work out.

More to the point, whether or not (as with Scrooge) your night dream was booted into being by "an undigested bit of undercooked potato," the associations you bring to that dream when you wake up *always* have meaning, just as your associations to anything in waking life have meaning. It doesn't finally matter what "causes" dreams (biology or psychology). What matters is what we make of them after we wake up.

There are actually many similarities between daydreams and night dreams. Dr. Rosalind Cartwright, who studies dreams at the sleep-disorder clinic of the Rush Presbyterian Hospital in Chicago, has found that some of the brain waves that occur during night dreams also occur during daydreams. Dr. Fiss and his colleagues have found that both kinds of dreams occur in the realm of the brain that is disconnected from physical activity. This is why they both usually occur without triggering an instant, related action. There are good reasons for this "disconnect"; soon we'll talk about what happens when you act on a daydream without giving yourself a chance to explore some of its less obvious meanings.

But to continue the comparison of daydreams and night dreams: Dr. Stephen Salker, one of the earliest researchers to make this comparison, found significant similarities in what he called the style of dreaming—specifically, the way in which your dreams represent your feelings. In other words, if your night dreams are symbolizing anxiety, your daydreams probably will as well. Or if in your daydreams you are dealing with depressive feelings, in all likelihood you will deal with the same concerns in your night dreams.

ALLOWING DAY- AND NIGHT DREAMS TO HELP EXPLAIN EACH OTHER

Because of these similarities, you can use many of the same tools to decipher both your daydreams and your night dreams. And because you are the author of both kinds, there are naturally going to be connections between the issues you struggle with in your daydreams and night dreams in the same period of time. The logical conclusion is that you can use your daydreams to help explain your night dreams—and, of course, vice versa.

For example, let's say you're unhappy at work. You don't know what to do about it, but you frequently have daydreams about getting a new job, winning the lottery, marrying a rich man or woman. Or you imagine yourself a brilliant scientist, nurtured and protected by your employers, who value your creative genius so much that they don't make you go to boring meetings and they never criticize you. Or perhaps you think about getting a job as a flight attendant, traveling all over the world, escaping from your demanding boss and difficult children.

In a night dream at the same time, you find yourself trapped in a room with no doors or windows. You're frightened. You don't know how to get out. Suddenly, you fly up out of the room. You've escaped! You're safe. Not only that, but the feeling of flying, of soaring over the rooftops, is exhilarating. You feel free, light, alive, and full of energy!

In this situation, both your daydreams and night dreams are about escaping from a situation in which you feel trapped. You know that you can't act on the night dream and just fly out of the situation. But the daydreams seem more realistic. You wonder: maybe you really should think about moving out of the city, getting a new job, doing something exciting and different, a little crazy.

However, *are* the daydreams necessarily more realistic than your night dreams? They obviously are more representative of something you could actually carry out in life. But would moving away—leaving your family—really solve your problems? Do you honestly believe that the life of an airline attendant, a pilot, a famous scientist would bring you a sense of satisfaction that isn't attainable in your current life?

If so, there are some questions you should ask yourself: What exactly about each option would alter your life and feelings? What would be different? Why can't you have those differences in your life as it is? The goal here isn't to convince yourself that Kansas is better than Oz—that everything you always wanted is in your own (current) backyard. The options your daydreams offer you can indeed light the way to a new life—even perhaps as a scientist or an airline attendant. But your daydreams, like your night dreams, are rarely important because of what psychologists call their "manifest" or surface content. They're important because of the associations, feelings, and meanings their content calls up in you. And whether fantastic or mundane, day- and night dreams can often illuminate what's going on in each other, just as they did in the hypothetical example above. Wishes for freedom, recognition, and creative excitement can be seen in both the night dreams of flying out of that room and the daydreams of being a brilliant scientist. Your greater understanding of yourself—culled from your subsequent thoughts and images—will help you understand how you unconsciously organize your life, what you experience about yourself and others that keeps you "stuck," makes you long for escape, and what you can do about it.

So much more goes on than meets the eye in both day- and night dreams. In James Thurber's classic story "The Secret Life of Walter Mitty," Mr. Mitty spends most of his time daydreaming. In "real life" a passive, ineffectual man married to a demanding and critical woman, Walter Mitty is always getting things wrong and is always in trouble. But in his secret life, his dream world, he is a powerful, even dangerous man, admired, respected, and feared by others. At one time he imagines himself a brilliant surgeon who not only saves a patient the other doctors cannot help, but also repairs a complicated anesthetic machine that no one else can fix. In another he imagines himself a fearless fighter pilot facing danger with a cool and composed fatalism. In each of these daydreams, Walter Mitty imagines that he is strong, competent, respected— the opposite of what he seems in real life.

But if I had Mr. Mitty as a client, I'd love to ask him: Why these images? Why a surgeon, a fighter pilot? What people come to his mind when he thinks about these characters? What do they mean to him? In his fantasies, does he finally earn his wife's approval and admiration? Why is she so critical of him? Why is he so passive with her? Is he afraid of her? Why? Just as important, do his daydreams irritate his wife? Is that, in fact, one of their indirect purposes? Does he drive her crazy when he gets so involved in his fantasies that he forgets to run her errands? I doubt if he thinks of himself as purposefully antagonizing her, but perhaps he gets some kind of unconscious revenge through his daydreams.

Unfortunately, we don't have any of Mitty's night dreams or his associations to work with. They most likely would convey the same issues his daydreams do and, put together with those daydreams, might answer some of my questions.

But how do the rest of us link our day- and night dreams? How can we learn from both, and how do they illuminate each other?

Kathryn, a thirty-five-year-old woman who attended one of

my daydream workshops, said that she hadn't paid much attention to her daydreams until she had a series of night dreams that she couldn't figure out. "Over the course of several months," she said, "I had a number of dreams about putting important papers in lockers and then losing the key. Or I would have the key but I couldn't remember the correct locker number. And sometimes I would get the right locker number and have the key but the papers wouldn't be in there. It was very dangerous, because these were important papers—if they fell into the wrong hands, something terrible would happen.

"When I was awake, I kept trying to figure out what the key symbolized. I knew that a key in a lock was supposed to be sexual, but that didn't fit with anything that was going on in my life as far as I could tell. I was going to just put it off as some weird leakage from my unconscious when it finally dawned on me that the terror that I was feeling in the dreams—the fear of losing something important—was an exaggerated version of how I was feeling in my waking life.

"I had been walking around in a daze for months. It had become a family joke that I'd said 'I'm losing my marbles' so often that my four-year-old daughter asked my husband where my marbles were and if they could go out and buy me some new ones.

"I was overwhelmed and overworked at my job. I was having *daydreams* of quitting, escaping to the Caribbean, becoming a beachcomber. But I just told myself, 'Everyone has those fantasies. Stop daydreaming and go back to work.'

"Now I saw that the night dreams and the daydreams were related to each other. What was important wasn't the lock and key, but the feeling of 'losing it' that they represented. Not only was I afraid of losing track of things, but I was also 'losing it' emotionally. I was losing my temper all the time, and I had said to my husband and my friends that I was losing my mind!

"Once I realized this, I decided that I actually needed to take some action about the problem. I couldn't keep going this way. I had a terrible conflict. I was trying to be 'Supermom'—to be a perfect mother and perfect in my job at the same time. My husband and I talked about what I really needed and wanted—which was both to be at home more and to continue to work in my profession. My husband has always been a very involved partner and parent, but in the end the child care and household affairs have always really been my responsibility.

"After our discussion, two things happened—one at home, the other at work. My husband agreed to cook dinner three times a week and take on a number of other household chores. My oldest son also offered to take on some extra chores, and now he cooks one night a week, too. All of which has freed me not only to do whatever job-related work I take home with me, but to *relax* more—hang out with my kids, enjoy myself more. At work, I talked to my boss about the fact that I needed an assistant. I laid out all of my reasons—emphasizing that it would help the productivity of our whole department, not just lessen the load for me. To my surprise, she agreed with me!

"It's made a huge difference. The nightmares about locks and keys have gone. And I only occasionally daydream about moving to the Caribbean. Life is still crazy and overwhelming, but it isn't impossible anymore. And if it gets that way again, I'll understand what's happening and figure out what I need to do about it a lot faster!"

Kathryn said that it took her several months to make these connections between what her night- and daydreams were telling her; once she had made them, she took some positive actions to ameliorate the problem she now saw had fueled each of those sets of dreams. And as she was able to acknowledge what was really troubling her, based on what her dreams were telling her, she became clearer about what she might do to make the problem more manageable. However, being moved to *act* isn't the necessary goal of examining your day- and night dreams and how they connect. The goal here is a greater clarity, a wider consciousness of the demons you're wrestling with, demons that may appear in various guises whether in your day- or night dreams. Once again, there can be great satisfaction in acknowledging *in words* the true nature of what's bothering you. The problem begins to feel more manageable. Sometimes achieving this consciousness is enough in itself; you may feel greater peace simply from knowing more precisely what you're actually grappling with, both internally and externally.

DECEPTIVE SIMPLICITY: CRACKING THE "SEEDS" OF DAY- AND NIGHT DREAMS

Certainly this was the case with Martin, a lawyer and family man in his fifties who was conscious that he was struggling with fears of growing older, but couldn't at first see the connection between his dreams and this conflict, even though he had a hunch somehow that the connection was there.

Martin was especially confounded by a very simple but potent dream he had the night before he came to see me. He dreamed that he was walking hand in hand with his high-school girlfriend, at night, along the beach. The mood was very peaceful; he felt deeply content just walking with the girl, listening to the soft sound of the surf, in the warm, dark, starlit night.

When he told me about the dream, he was concerned that it might have something to do with his marriage. "We have the standard marital tiffs," Martin said, "but we're both pretty happy with each other. I love my wife very much, and I know she loves me, too." He went on in a puzzled voice. "I haven't thought about that girl in years. I can't imagine why I dreamt about her."

I suggested he might be able to throw some light on the

night dream by examining what was going on in his daydreams at the time. Daydreams often give a more direct reflection of the frame of concerns in the here and now. Since he'd had his girl-friend dream the night before he spoke to me, I asked him what images and thoughts were occurring to him today. "Tell me any-thing that comes to your mind right now," I said.

"Well, I was back in my hometown this weekend, visiting my mother. That's where I met this girl thirty years ago, before I'd met my wife. I passed the hospital where my father had been when he'd had his first heart trouble—the girl in the dream worked there—that's where we met. Oh, and I remember briefly thinking about her at that moment." This information is what dream analysts call "day residue"—experiences in your waking life that may have triggered some of the ideas or images in the dream you have that night.

Dr. Singer, that pioneer in the study of daydreams, takes this idea even further. He suggests that night dreams actually begin life as daydreams. His idea is that we have so many distractions during the day that we can't pay attention to our dreams until we go to sleep and can focus on them more thoroughly. Though not everyone who studies dreams agrees with Dr. Singer on this, there is general agreement that both daydreams and night dreams are triggered by the same issues—our waking interests and worries.

I asked Martin to tell me more about his thoughts and feel-ings over the weekend. "It was a hard visit. My mom's always been so independent. Ever since my dad died, she's been on her own. But what we've all dreaded has finally happened. She really can't stay by herself any longer. She's gotten forgetful. I don't think she's eating—there was hardly anything in her refrigerator or her cabinets. And she can't drive anymore, so someone's got to come at least to take her grocery-shopping. But what's even more disturbing is that she seems to forget that she's got something cooking on the stove. Several of her pots were burned to a crisp, and when I asked her about it she just sort of laughed it off. That's never happened before, and I'm worried that she'll end up burning the house down and herself with it.

"Now my sister and I have to make some decisions. And Mom's going to hate any of them—whether we insist she have someone in the house with her full-time, or whether we move her to a residence of some sort. It's not going to be easy for any of us."

Although at first he wasn't aware of it, these thoughts were associations to the dream. Through them, we would get closer to the symbolic meaning, the coded message of the dream.

Martin said that, when he'd visited his mother, he'd done a lot of reminiscing. As he drove around his hometown, he passed numerous personal landmarks. He walked around the campus of the high school he and his sister had attended. He drove back to the house he had grown up in. He noted the store where he had had his first job, and the basketball court where he had taken part in countless pickup games. And he passed the hospital where his father spent his last days. He told me, "That's where I met her—the girl in the dream. I didn't date her very long. I was home from college, visiting my father in the hospital—it was after he'd had his first heart attack. She was a nurse in training at the hospital. She was changing Dad's IV. I teased her about getting it right; she was a good sport about it. We dated while I was home, and then a few times when I came home to visit after that. Then she wrote me that she was getting engaged. We'd never been that serious, so I wasn't upset or anything. But I appreciated her being so honest with me—writing to me. She could have waited until I called her, the next time I came home. It was nice of her to let me know ahead of time."

"So you have pleasant feelings about her?" I asked.

"Yeah. She helped me through a difficult time. And she was even nice after it was over—after my father got out of the hospital."

I repeated his words: "She helped you through a difficult

time—and she was even nice after it was over." Martin was quiet. "Is it possible you're longing for someone to do that for you now?"

"Funny that you should put it that way. I guess that's just what I've been wanting." Martin was going through a difficult time right now, not only dealing with his mother but confronting the fact that he was growing older. He hadn't realized until he heard his own words—and applied them directly to the here and now, what he was feeling today—that his dream was a coded message of *longing*—for someone to pay attention to him the way this girl had done so many years before.

It took my repeating his own words to him to help him make this connection, but he soon realized that he also had the power—as the rest of us do—to repeat his own words to himself, making possibly illuminating associations to what was going on in his life right at that moment. This is one of the great benefits of putting your thoughts into words. Sometimes all you have to do is hear yourself say them out loud and the framework becomes clear. This can also happen when you read something you've written: it can seem different, clearer and more meaningful than the thought was before you translated it into words.

Of course, there are times when we can't "hear" or "read" our own words so clearly, and may need someone else (in Martin's case it was me, his therapist, but it might just as easily have been a friend or a colleague) to repeat to us what we've said. Decoding our own words is usually a groping and imperfect process; we all have blind spots, and it can help to get some perspective about our own words from someone else.

But now that Martin had begun to translate some of the symbolic meanings of his nighttime dream into words, he had also begun to pay attention to some of the painful feelings and thoughts that he had been trying to push away during his visit with his mother. This is one of the reasons we put information into code in both our daydreams and night dreams: they contain feelings that make us uncomfortable, feelings that exist but that we try to keep out of view.

Furthermore, it isn't unusual to keep more than one set of feelings out of awareness, and therefore for one dream—day or night—to represent more than one group of uncomfortable feelings. Martin confided that, when he returned to his high school, he had daydreamed about his triumphs on the basketball courts and his days working at the store, his pride in himself for making and saving money for the first time in his life. In the light of the associations he'd already made about his night dream of his girlfriend, he now realized he was daydreaming—as well as night-dreaming—about, and mourning, his lost youth. In other words, in his day- as well as night dreams, Martin had managed temporarily to roll the clock back—to return to a time when he was young, his father was still alive, and his mother was vital and healthy. By going back to that time, Michael could avoid—at least temporarily—unpleasant and difficult feelings about his mother's future and his own.

The dream about his nurse/girlfriend symbolized another group of feelings that Martin was avoiding. As we talked, it became clear to both of us that he was angry and upset with his wife and his sister for not being more concerned about his mother and more supportive of him. Although he loved his wife and they generally got along quite well, he was also hurt and angry at her unsympathetic attitude toward her mother-in-law. Indirectly and unconsciously, through the dream, Martin took revenge on her by imagining himself with someone who he believed would have been more sympathetic to *his* plight.

An abundance of information about ourselves is packed into both day- and night dreams; as we saw with Martin, it takes patience with yourself, and sometimes outside help as well, to begin to sort out the strands of this information from the often deceptive dream symbols in which they are invisibly meshed. Sometimes, perhaps bafflingly, you learn that your dreams can function to reinforce negative feelings about yourself. We'll go into this in greater depth later on, but since you may very well be banging into some of this self-bashing early on, as you do the preliminary exercises in this book and begin to think more deeply about the meaning of your day- and night dreams, an introductory word is apt right here.

Evelyn, a professional women in her mid-forties, demonstrates this strange phenomenon vividly. After struggling through an unpleasant divorce and a painful move to a new home, Evelyn had pulled her life together and was feeling stronger and even happier than she had in years. Then she had this night dream: "I was going to a party. Everyone ignored me. I felt completely rejected. Then I had to go to work. The party was at my office, and I had to walk through it to get to my desk. I felt terrible. Then I thought, 'It's all right. I can do my work and they can keep on partying.' Somehow that seemed to make me feel better, and I got my work done."

Evelyn's first thought about this dream was: "I'll never make new friends. I'll always feel left out." But she had already done some work on her dreams, and she had learned to ask what all of us should ask about our own dreams: "Why did I create this story?" She allowed herself to feel what the dream brought up in her, and she surprised herself with a sudden revelation. "Being rejected in that dream—I feel so very familiar with that feeling of rejection. It seems very natural to me." But Evelyn couldn't relate this feeling to what she was going through in her current life. She had lately been, as she put it, "full of myself"—more happy with and connected to the people in her life, both her family and colleagues at work, than she'd felt in a long time—the opposite of rejected. "It's like I've had a personality transplant. I'm just not used to feeling accepted, I guess: I wonder where this new me came from!" In her dream she had painted a reality that was painful, but familiar—a reality that seemed on some level to be the "truth" about her. Her phrase "personality transplant" was significant: she felt as though this period of happiness had somehow been grafted onto her, had come from outside her; it wasn't the real Evelyn.

I suggested that she had decided in this dream to get back to her old self, which seemed to have soothed her. She agreed—and realized with new force that this new "happiness" in her life made her uncomfortable. "Just yesterday I remember thinking to myself, 'Now, don't get too big for your britches!' I guess I was trying to bring myself down. And I did it in my dream." She then recognized that telling herself not to get too big for her britches was, in fact, a daydream—for that fleeting moment, she imagined herself as overbearing and overconfident and foolish. Her day- and night dreams meshed; they illuminated the pull in her to go back to her painful but familiar (and therefore to some degree soothing) old "rejected" self. On the heels of this realization, another thought occurred to Evelyn: she realized she was playing out in her head the dire consequences of being too happy. "I was just thinking about another time that I let myself feel good. I ended up getting kicked in the teeth as a result!"

Both her day- and her night dreams were responses to Evelyn's unfamiliar good feelings about herself. Although these new feelings were exhilarating, they made her feel vulnerable. Warning herself internally not to get too excited was a reminder that her good feelings left her unprotected, and that she'd better not let her guard down. Apparently, her daydream, the first try, didn't quite work, since she continued to feel good for the rest of the day. But her anxiety did not go away, so in her night dream she intensified the fight, not only reminding herself that she would eventually be rejected, but also trying to convince herself that she was perfectly comfortable with rejection anyway, that this rejected self was the "real" Evelyn.

When she realized that both her daydreams and her night

dream were attempts at self-protection, she was able to acknowledge: "Okay, I know I don't like feeling vulnerable. But I feel
vulnerable when I feel rejected, too! Maybe I'll work on trying to
feel *good* and vulnerable instead of *bad* and vulnerable for a while."
Evelyn's dreams represented the difficulty she had integrating new
feelings about herself, but they also heralded a change; the conflict
they embodied was in fact a sign of exciting new developments in
her personality.

DREAMS AS ATTEMPTS TO WORK
THROUGH PROBLEMS

Feelings we don't want to face head-on are often encoded into
our day- and night dreams. But as we've seen with both Martin
and Evelyn, we can also interpret this self-protective "encoding"
as the psyche's attempt to *manage* difficult feelings—in a sense, to
resolve them. Indeed, in his research, Dr. Fiss has found that night
dreams, just like daydreams, help us to work through difficult
situations, adapt to others, and communicate hidden information
to ourselves, as well as express unacceptable feelings. He has also
found that night dreams, like daydreams, most often represent
waking concerns and preoccupations. In a series of studies, he and
his colleagues concluded that, if you pay attention to your night
dreams, even if you don't understand what they mean, you will
enhance not only your self-awareness, but also your ability to
solve problems and cope with life's difficulties.

Is there a way we can make this problem-solving potential in
our dreams more conscious? Can we *use* the information in our
dreams to begin to solve problems, as Evelyn was able to do?

The following two-part exercise will help.

EXERCISE:

USING YOUR NIGHT DREAMS TO SOLVE PROBLEMS

PART I

Pull out your daydream notebook and a pen and put them on your night table, or somewhere accessible to your bed. For the next week, keep a record of the dreams you remember from your sleep. Don't worry if all you can remember is a fragment of a dream, or if a night or two go by without any dream memories at all. Eventually, if you simply suggest to yourself that you want to remember your dreams and write down what you can remember in your notebook, your dream memories should become more regular and detailed.

Don't think you have to write pages and pages about each dream. A few sentences, even a few words, capturing the key ideas are enough. If you wake up in the middle of the night remembering a dream, write it down immediately—don't tell yourself you'll remember it when you wake up in the morning (nine times out of ten, you won't). If you hate the idea of writing, keep a tape recorder by your bed and record your dreams on it. Try telling someone else about your dreams each day. Ask your friend not to analyze: the purpose is simply for you to put your dreams into words, which will help you remember more about the gist and content of the dreams.

PART II

1. You may find that simply writing down your dreams, recording them, or reciting them to someone else will give you a

different perspective on them. Sometimes putting them into words will even give you some preliminary interpretations.

But to go a little further toward understanding your dream symbols, take another moment to write down any of the components of the dream (an image, a person, a question asked, or statement made) that seem odd or stand out. Then notice any thoughts or ideas that occur to you as you think of these elements.

2. Ask yourself the questions we've been asking about daydreams:

a. What is the story or narrative that I am telling myself in this dream?

b. Why am I telling myself this story? What do I hope to accomplish with it?

c. Why am I telling it to myself now? What is going on in my life that makes it relevant?

As with your daydreams, write down *anything* that occurs to you. It's unlikely that you'll be able to write simple, definitive answers to any of these questions. Even if the answer that occurs to you seems way out in left field, write it down, and think about it. See what thoughts come to you: try hard not to censor what may at first seem to be silly connections.

How will all of this help you to solve problems? According to Dr. James Fosshage, a New York City psychologist and author, night dreams help us organize, synthesize, and represent unarticulated information about ourselves. By putting your dreams—day and night—into words and asking yourself these questions, you will begin to make connections to some of the underlying, indirect, or distorted meanings of these internal communications. As you have probably already begun to see, the more practice you get letting your thoughts flow in this way, the more interesting ideas will occur to you—and the more of a handle you will get on the connections your dreams (day and night) make to your daily life.

These links can help you base your decisions and actions more clearly on what you're finding out you really want. This doesn't always translate into concrete action. Martin's consciousness that he was afraid of growing old and angry at his wife for not caring more about his mother simply allowed him to understand better what he was really feeling. The point wasn't especially to get him to "act" differently—merely to acknowledge that he felt more than he was letting himself realize. The benefit to him is that his anxiety has lessened; now that uncomfortable feelings he had not been able to think about have come to light, he's experienced a sense of wholeness, even a greater buoyancy, and a feeling of wisdom vis-à-vis the challenges he faces in his daily life. For Evelyn, however, her understanding did translate to a kind of new "action"—or at least a change of attitude. She is able now more consciously to *choose* to feel "good and vulnerable" instead of "bad and vulnerable." She has begun to let her personality grow and change with less impediment now that—thanks to her day- and night dreams—she knows more about the "unthought" fear of change that had been her unconscious guide.

Let's turn now to some specific types of daydreams—and examples of how people have used them to understand themselves. Remember that you can ask yourself each of the questions I ask to move the process along with each person I am describing—to open up the messages contained in *your* internal monologues.

Part Two

B Y   N O W   Y O U have a sense of how your daydreams, these fascinating windows into your psyche, work. You know that they help you to process and organize experience, solve problems, rehearse for upcoming events; that they often do this silently, without your knowledge or conscious participation; and that they can tell you about some of the unrecognized assumptions around which you organize many of your actions, thoughts, and decisions.

How can you use this newfound awareness, derived from your daydreams, to resolve problems in your daily life? How can you put your daydreams to work at your job, in your friendships, love life, family life? This is where our path leads next. In the following chapters, you will journey further into the world of self-knowledge, with your daydreams as both vehicle and avenue. The real-life examples and exercises in these chapters will help you understand and make use of these fascinating signals from your internal world. Keep in mind, however, that your experience is your own; though your images and even your struggles may be the same as those in some of the examples, the symbols are *yours*. As I've said throughout the book, the same symbol may mean one thing for you and something completely different for someone else. You've learned the basic tool of allowing your thoughts to go their own direction, and then trying to find the stories and themes in those wanderings. The exercises in these chapters will heighten your ability to find your own special meanings in the images of your daydreams.

Some of your daydreams do represent your "real" goals: directions you want to go, accomplishments you want to achieve. Of course, we now know that the goals they represent are not always the most obvious ones. But in this section we will examine your daydreams for coded clues to what your real goals are, and to the path to reach them. And we will also mine your daydreams for information about how you interfere with your own progress, for ways you shoot yourself in the foot and keep yourself from achieving the very things you long for. In the next chapters, we'll explore ways to use your daydreams to solve these problems and, in the process, simultaneously move closer to your real goals. None of this is simple, which is why meaningful personal change rarely happens overnight. But through the growing self-awareness you are developing as you explore your daydreams, you will be able to turn the prism just a little; and the slight shift in your per-spective—in your understanding of your own experience and your view of your behavior patterns—can make an astounding difference in your life.

CHAPTER SIX

Out of the Clear Blue Sky: Using Your Daydreams at Work

RACHEL, WHO FOR many years ran a progressive school for elementary- and junior-high-age children, was always proud of the school's unconventional teaching methods. Kids were grouped by abilities and interests, not solely by age or "grade." The energy-and-activity level was always high. You had the impression that the children in this school never stopped for a minute, they were so busy and absorbed in their schoolwork. But once, when a famous actor looked in on his own child's classroom, he turned to the teacher and said, "It worries me to see all these kids so busy concentrating on their schoolwork." The teacher stared at him, astonished: the energy and involvement of the children were a selling point of the school. The actor went on: "When I was a kid, I was bored stiff in school. I spent all my time daydreaming. And those daydreams are where I got the inspiration for most of the work I've done in my life."

The actor was only half joking. His story conveys the understanding that daydreams are moments for turning inward, communicating with yourself, trying on different ideas and feelings, even different identities. In your daydreams you can turn reality upside down and inside out. You can think about what you don't know, imagine and explore what you've never felt, and see things from a different, uncharacteristic perspective.

This shifting of perspective is the basis for what social psychologists call "creative problem-solving"—the capacity to allow our minds to flow through their own random and sometimes confusing channels until we find a solution to a difficulty. Creative problem-solving often involves turning a situation upside down or on its side, so that, by viewing it from a totally different angle, we can open up the potential to find a previously unseen resolution.

Of course it's no surprise to think that certain kinds of jobs are all about creative problem-solving; but have you ever thought that that's what you do in your own work? Don't immediately write off the possibility just because you think of your job as mundane or boring. As you'll see later in this chapter, you may lack interest in your daily activities precisely because you close off aspects of your own creative potential, and this lack of interest may in turn contribute to that very closing off of your creativity. One of the issues we'll discuss in this chapter is how to use your daydreams to tap into that elusive—and engrossing—creative part of yourself in your work life.

To begin with, it's crucial to recognize that, no matter what you do, whether you are a secretary or an accountant, a stockbroker or a schoolteacher, a cashier, a lawyer, or a homemaker, you face and solve problems of one sort or another every day. They may seem minor, and maybe you've never thought of yourself as being particularly creative about them. But you already have this ability. And once you know how to take command of your existing capability, you can capitalize on it by using your daydreams to deal with troubles beyond your normal problem-solving abilities.

"FRUIT BASKET TURN OVER": SOLVING PROBLEMS BY SHIFTING PERSPECTIVES

Jennifer was in her forties, a successful computer programmer who worked at a large financial firm. Because the company was downsizing, her own and her immediate boss's jobs were at risk. She had never felt particularly supported by this man, but he was getting worse during the crisis. Jennifer explained: "He's under a lot of pressure. It's a hard time for all of us, but I think he's worried more than the rest of us. I mean, I'm worried too—I'm the main breadwinner in my family. But I have pretty marketable skills, and I figure I can always find *something*. And I don't have to keep up my male ego like he does. In the current market, he'll have a hard time finding another job at the same level and with the same salary he's got now. But, still, even if I was *really* upset, I'd never do what he's doing: taking it out on the rest of us. He's negative and hostile, not to mention completely unsupportive." To make matters worse, the project they were working on had hit a snag. Neither she nor any of her staff could figure out how to get around the problem. "And," she told me, "my boss doesn't have anything even slightly helpful to add. The only thing he has to say—and he has plenty of it—is critical."

One morning she forced herself to go out for a jog before work, even though it meant getting up extra early. As she ran, her thoughts drifted: first to the brilliantly blue sky and the crisp, sparkling air; then to her sense of smug self-satisfaction about getting up and exercising before her colleagues were even awake; and then to a brief debate with herself about whether or not she could have a jelly doughnut as a reward for burning all those extra calories! Her thoughts touched momentarily on the workday ahead of her, and then, for no reason she could name, she started to think about her college roommate. As she puffed along, she grinned with pleasure remembering a number of youthful, slightly irresponsible escapades the two of them had gotten into. One in particular had created quite an uproar, when Jennifer and her roommate moved their furniture around after midnight one night, trying to make their cramped dorm room more livable, and completely forgetting that the resident adviser lived immediately below them. The next day, they were called into the dean's office and told they had to write a letter of apology to the adviser. Jennifer grinned more broadly as she remembered the gales of laughter that had accompanied their first (unapologetic and unsent) attempts to write that letter.

Later that day, Jennifer again thought of the incident. She began to pay attention to the thoughts that followed the image; as she did so, she noticed an important theme that ran through many of these connections. As a result, Jennifer realized that the daydream that had seemed to come "out of the clear blue sky" contained a significant clue to the solution to her work problem. First, she saw that if she rearranged some of the factors involved (as she and her roommate had done with their dormitory furniture) the answer became practically self-evident. At the same time, she realized that she had been ignoring another critical piece of internal information. "It was like this game my first-grade teacher used to play. At some time during the day, she would call 'fruit basket

turn over,' and all of us would have to change seats. It was chaos;
but it got us to sit beside kids other than the ones we always sat
with, and although to us kids it just seemed like great fun, it
always made it easier to concentrate on our work or listen to what
she was saying. By turning things around, I would be shifting the
status quo—openly disagreeing with my boss, who is convinced
that the answer can be found in the setup we've already got. I
don't know why, since he's been so critical of me recently, but I
feel uncomfortable criticizing *him*. But I know I'm right. We've
got to change things around to solve this problem."

I asked Jennifer to tell me the first images that came to her
mind when she thought about criticizing her superior. "Well, I
can imagine his face. He'll look embarrassed, maybe humiliated."
She chuckled, then immediately looked serious. "I'm not a
vengeful person, you understand"—perhaps reassuring herself as
much as me—"but the truth is, he deserves it. It would be an
understatement to say that he hasn't been supportive of me." She
was silent for a moment, then said, "You know, I was just
thinking about my resident adviser again. I haven't ever thought
about this before, but she was a very judgmental person. My
roommate and I wouldn't have purposefully disturbed her, but I
didn't really mind that our little prank woke her up that night.
She almost deserved it for being so disapproving and negative
about everything we did."

Jennifer had used almost the same words when she described
her boss's behavior. Once she noted the similarity of her feelings
about the two people—her boss and her resident adviser—she was
on the verge of learning something that she didn't particularly like
about herself: that she did have a "vengeful" streak. Her refusal to
acknowledge that she might want to get back at her boss had contributed to her inability to come up with a solution: the answer to
her problem included a little touch of revenge. Once she *had* recognized this suppressed facet of her personality, she was freer to

use her entire self in the problem-solving process, which led to a creative solution.

This is one of the benefits—and "dangers"—of exploring your daydreams. You'll find out a lot more about yourself, but you may not always like everything you learn. Just remember: we're all made up of many different characteristics, some likable, some not. Don't fall into the trap of defining yourself on the basis of any single quality. The more facets of yourself you can allow into your awareness, the more choices you'll have; and the more solutions.

In their complex way, daydreams both conceal and reveal our multidimensional selves. We've talked about how you may keep frightening or disturbing feelings at bay in order to protect yourself from difficult, painful, or overwhelming emotions. As we've just seen, these pushed-away feelings may be about something you're ashamed of or embarrassed by—like Jennifer's vengefulness. But you can pay a hefty price for not knowing about feelings that you don't approve of: not only do you limit your options in any problem-solving situation, as Jennifer did, but you may also limit your ability to know about and work toward whatever dreams you might really want to accomplish.

For example, you've always dreamed of going to medical school, but one thing and another has gotten in your way. Now you tell yourself that you're too far along another career track, too committed to your family, too old. But maybe you didn't even try for medical school because doctors have so much power, and you were afraid of—couldn't let yourself imagine—having that much power yourself. You can't get to this information easily: in reality, you would have to follow the long and winding road of your random (but connecting) thoughts to get to it. But once there, you will have access to other daydreams about your own power— and lack of it. You can now begin the process of sorting through your conflicts about having power, being powerless, being in someone else's power. And based on your growing understanding of your own fears and conflicts, you will be able to make new decisions about your goals. You will be freer to play with possibilities that had not occurred to you before. Perhaps you will decide that after all you want to go to medical school, even at your age. Or you may begin to think of other careers that will be still more satisfying and easier to move into.

Another of our capabilities that is curbed when our whole self isn't available to us, when there are qualities or feelings or aspects of who we are that we keep under wraps, is the ability to be interested in what we're doing. If you feel bored at work, chronically uninterested, and unable to do anything about it, this may well be a signal that you are keeping some aspect of yourself out of the picture.

"NOTHING VENTURED, NOTHING GAINED"

A tall, slender woman whose clear complexion and long silky blond hair made her look younger than her actual age of thirty-nine, Andrea had never found a job that really captured her interest. She was selling shoes when I met her, but she had worked in publishing, banking, and real estate since graduating from college. She hated her current job. "My boss is always on my case," she told me angrily. "She wants me to do more, but I already do more than anybody else at that damned place. I bust my ass, but I don't get any credit."

Andrea wanted to leave the job, but she didn't know what she should do next. "My God. I'm getting close to forty. I have to settle down," she told me. "What do you think I ought to do?"

When I asked about her daydreams, she snapped, "I don't have any."

I pushed on: "You don't think about what kind of job you'd like, or where you'll start looking if you quit this job? You don't think about whether to quit first and then see what you can find, or to look for work and then leave?"

"No. If they keep treating me like shit, I'll leave whether I have another job or not. And I'll find something else. That's not a daydream. It's a fact."

"Do you think about how they'd react if you left?" I asked.

"Nope. They won't care. Staff like me's a dime a dozen. Or so they think. They'll regret it when they find out that nobody else will do as much of their shit work as I do, but that's not a daydream, either. It's a fact."

Although Andrea called these ideas "facts," she had actually told me several daydreams. Besides the self-fulfilling daydream/plan that she would get so "ticked off" that she would simply leave the job, Andrea was also daydreaming that her boss would finally recognize how hard she actually worked.

Andrea was resistant to the idea that her thoughts were only one version of a possible reality (which is, of course, what a daydream is). But I suspected that this resistance was part of why she was unable to find work that excited her. I wondered why she kept herself so locked into one way of thinking about her life. Her daydreams, which might have helped her get more involved in her work, were completely unavailable to her. But before we could find the keys to her inner world, we would have to explore and understand what made her so reluctant—perhaps afraid?—even to know about her fantasy life. I asked her to tell me what she thought about daydreams, any associations she had to the concept itself.

"I don't daydream," she insisted. "I'm not going to think about something that won't come true. Why would anybody do that to themselves?"

"Do that to themselves?" I asked, interested that she would frame the idea of a daydream in this way.

"Yeah. I mean, why bother?" she demanded. "You only

end up being disappointed." This reaction—a valuable clue—told me that Andrea connected daydreaming with disappointment. I asked her to tell me what came to her mind when she thought about being disappointed.

"It's simple," she said. "I remember the last time I ever let myself feel it. I think about it a lot, so that I won't ever let something like this happen to me again. My parents got divorced when I was eight. I was glad. Our house had been hell with their fights. I thought now we'd have some peace." She laughed bitterly. "How wrong can you be? They loved to hate each other. And it spilled over onto us kids. Or maybe they just hated everybody, us included. Anyway, one day my dad took my brother and me for our weekly visit. He'd promised us a trip to a toy store, and we'd been planning for it all week. My brother built and collected model airplanes, and he knew exactly what model he was going to get. I was going to wait. I wanted to see what was there, savor the possibilities, make a choice then. We got to the store, and my brother went right to the models and picked one out. But I was walking around, checking out the stuffed animals, the dolls, the puzzles. I was having a wonderful time; but after what seemed like an incredibly short time, my father got fed up and told me I had to make a choice—immediately. I was getting ready to; I had decided on a beautiful fat stuffed panda bear. But I didn't do it fast enough, and he yelled at me that I had taken too long, that I wasn't going to get anything at all. He said I'd ruined both of our chances, that he wasn't going to buy my brother's plane, either, and he dragged us both out of there, my brother deathly white and completely silent, me sobbing and begging every painful step of the way. It was the most godawful thing I've ever experienced in my life. I don't know if you can imagine it . . . but I decided then and there never to count on anything—or anyone—ever again. And I haven't."

This painful memory was an example of something Freud

called a "screen memory"—an image that represents more than just a memory. Not everyone keeps hurtful experiences active, as Andrea did, but when we do, it is often a way of trying to protect ourselves from the difficult feelings these experiences reflect. (Sometimes *forgetting* experiences can serve a similar purpose.) Andrea probably *had* felt disappointment during the years after this incident, but she employed the memory as a conscious reminder to keep herself from hoping for anything from another person.

"It sounds horrible," I said when she had finished. "Although perhaps your father's version of the story would tell us something different—something you wouldn't have known about as a child. Still, I can certainly understand why you would never want to feel like that again."

We talked some more about how Andrea's closing off all desires was her attempt to protect herself against possible repeat of that terrible feeling, but then I pointed out that this protective device didn't always succeed. In fact, the very mechanism that she used to keep disappointment at bay also kept her in a constant state of discontent. "What do you mean?" she demanded. I explained that she didn't let herself get interested in anything for the same reason she didn't let herself daydream—to keep herself from feeling disappointed—but that she also kept herself from feeling involved, energized, excited by anything.

Andrea was not impressed, but I encouraged her to let herself digest the idea. Several weeks later, she said, "I was thinking about what you said—that I'm actually *always* disappointed. And I started to wonder what that feels like. How do I know if I'm disappointed? And how do I cope with it?"

Andrea was starting to face one of the feelings that she had been trying to push away all her life. The first, most important step toward being able to cope with these feelings, as we saw with Ellie as she grieved for her dying mother, is often to try to put them into words. However, this is not as easy as it may sound, partly because putting your feelings into words does not make them go away. As Dr. Demos has learned in her work with children, naming an emotion can make it seem worse at first. Many times, however, simply *sitting with* a feeling that you have put into words will allow it to resolve itself. It is often when we try not to feel something that we get stuck in that very feeling. Andrea had begun to see that she had been tolerating disappointment all her life, even though she had been trying to convince herself that she never felt it.

This was a new perspective on an old problem; shortly after we discussed it, Andrea found a new daydream beginning to emerge. "I can feel myself fighting it," she told me. "I feel like I've been taken back to that toy store. I start to think about which toys I like, which ones I might want; and then it's like I slap my hand and say to myself, 'You stupid-ass kid. You're going to get all excited, make your choice, and end up with nothing.'"

As Andrea struggled with her fears of being disappointed, she reminded herself that she had in fact tolerated a variety of disappointments throughout her life. I suggested she try to imagine what she would do now if she were suddenly, painfully, and traumatically disappointed. Her first response was, "I wouldn't put myself in that position." After thinking awhile, however, she came up with several possible scenes; and then, a little surprised at her own thoughts, she said, "I guess there's a major difference between me now and me as a little girl. I have a lot more say about what happens to me. I can pick myself up and start in another direction. I can tell people—even my dad—to fuck off. And I can even buy myself that panda if I want. I couldn't do any of that when I was a kid."

Andrea was slowly, anxiously opening up her daydream world. She imagined going back to the toy store of her childhood and buying herself a panda. "I don't really need to do it," she said slowly one day, "but I need to know that I can if I want to. Is that what daydreaming is about?"

For Andrea, that daydream heralded a new way of coping

with disappointment. And as a result, she was able to begin to explore some of her interests. She imagined opening a store of her own, "but I'd have to ask my father for help with the financing; and I'm not about to get into that struggle with him. Forget it."

I asked if she was stopping herself from daydreaming because she was afraid of being disappointed.

With a grin, she nodded yes. "Absolutely. But as soon as you asked me about it, another daydream flashed into my head. Maybe I don't have to ask my father for money. My brother might be willing to make me a loan. Even my mom might lend me a little."

As we've seen, many of our behaviors are based on assumptions that we don't even know we're making—silent beliefs that organize our actions and influence our decisions. Andrea's assumption that she would be disappointed was not silent; her belief that she could not bear the feeling was. Like Patricia, who had unquestionably adopted her family's myth that no one liked to socialize with people outside the family, Andrea began to see that neither of her assumptions was always true: she was not always disappointed, but when she was, she was not devastated by the feeling, as she had been as a child. "It's always felt so huge—final-like. I never thought I could feel disappointed and keep going anyway. Now I do. I say to myself, 'So you're disappointed. Okay. That's not the end of anything. Keep going and see what you feel next.' That's a new idea for me."

If you, too, are stuck in a job because of your fears of being disappointed, you can ask yourself the question Andrea was now asking: "How can I *handle* this feeling?" As Andrea discovered that she could live through disappointment without being destroyed by it, she found herself working harder at her job. "I didn't think I could work harder; but now I see that the reason it felt so hard was that I was always keeping part of myself out of the work so that I wouldn't be disappointed. It was pretty subtle, how I was doing it. But now I realize that I wouldn't bring out extra possible shoes, even if I had an idea of what a customer was looking for, because I hate that feeling of bringing out one pair of shoes after another, only to have the customer walk out without anything and leave me with a pile of boxes." But now that disappointment wasn't so frightening to her, Andrea found that she could both hear and respond to what her customers wanted. She began to make more sales and started getting more positive feedback from her boss. "I don't want to sell shoes the rest of my life," she told me firmly, "but I'm learning some good lessons while I'm doing it: lessons that will help me when I open my own store."

It isn't at all clear that Andrea will follow through on her dream of having her own store; now that her daydream world is accessible to her, who knows what other fantasies, or options, may open up. But the fact that she has a choice, that she sees possibilities where once she saw none, has had a powerful impact on her: she now feels interested in her work, engaged in her everyday tasks, in a way she never before imagined possible.

Andrea's goals were vague, often reactive to her fears and to an unpleasant or difficult situation instead of to her innermost wishes. As we saw, getting in touch with some of those fears released information about her wishes, so that she could start the process of developing some of her daydreams into realistic goals for herself. Sometimes you think you know exactly what your goals are but you can't seem to work toward them. Your day-dreams may even be interfering with your ability to achieve the very things you dream of. But by putting into practice some of the fundamentals we've been talking about all along—by paying attention to different components of your daydreams, by looking for themes and stories in apparently "free-floating" ideas—you can figure out what the interference is about. You'll be freer to work toward your dreams; or you may end up discovering other goals that you never knew about. You may change directions, follow other dreams. Things may seem more complex when you're finished, but the complexity has been there all along. When you don't see it, life can feel two-dimensional. Recognizing and examining the complexity of feelings, wishes, goals—and, yes, daydreams—is what adds richness to life. And it puts you in a position of strength. You may have more choices, more decisions to make. But the choices will be clearer, and at least you'll be able to get out of your own way as you set yourself meaningful goals, explore options, move forward, and even change directions.

DAYDREAMS OF PERFECTION

A tall, burly man with a shining bald pate, Ed had taught high-school English in the New York City public-school system for nearly twenty years. He was dedicated to his work and his students, and even felt that sometimes he made a difference in some of his pupils' lives. Still, he had a secret dream: to write for the movies. His mind was full of daydreams, some of which he thought would make good scripts. But something always seemed to stop him from actually putting his ideas into writing. As he put it, "I have legitimate excuses—grading papers, cleaning my apartment, doing things with my kids, spending time with my wife—but I also waste a lot of time when I could be writing."

I asked Ed if he could jot down some of his daydream ideas in a notebook. He wasn't sure, but he thought he might be able to make a few notes, as long as he didn't have to write out a whole story. Since, as you know, a daydream diary is made up of notes, not full stories, this plan could work well. Ed's daydreams ran the gamut from plots for the movies he wanted to write to which actors would perform in his movies. He imagined accepting his first Oscar; in fact, he had a daydream about the speech he would make and the people he would thank in that speech.

One of Ed's difficulties was immediately clear. His expectations were sky-high, too high for him to reach on his first efforts.

He took his fantasies of perfection literally, which paralyzed him. He had no idea how to start writing a script, since every word had to be Oscar material. There was no room for him to make a mistake, no space where he could be human (which, by definition, is to be imperfect). How could he possibly write down any of his ideas under this sort of pressure?

I suggested that we try an experiment. Could Ed write a beginner's script, one that could not possibly be produced? "You mean, take small steps? Not bite off such a big task all at once?" he replied. "Funny. That's what I tell my students all the time. I don't know why I never applied it to myself."

This wasn't as simple as it might sound, but Ed worked at it. And while he did, he continued to keep his daydream notebook. Eventually, he came in with a script about a man who dreamed of writing movies. And along with the script came a revelation. "I wrote this sort of tongue-in-cheek," he said. "This guy keeps writing movies in his head and gets lost in each scenario. And the movie is just one fantasy after another. It doesn't have a very good plot; I wouldn't send it out to anyone. But I finished it! And I realized as I was writing it that what might be interesting to write about is some of what I'm *really* seeing and living." Ed had always imagined action movies along the lines of James Bond or *The Godfather*, but now he said, "I could write about the life of a New York City public-school teacher. There's plenty of street action right here. I mean, we have a metal detector at the door to screen out the guns and knives these kids bring to school: that says plenty about the potential for violence, doesn't it? And there's lots of more subtle, touching stuff going on at the same time. I know these kids inside out. I see their pain and their anger and their frustration every day. And I know what it's like to reach through all of that and touch them, too. And it happens plenty. I could write about some of that." He stopped and grinned sheepishly. "As long as I don't get carried away with it. You know, I read an article about Kevin Costner, who I really admire. He's not a great actor or a great director, but he stays in there. He seems to really enjoy what he's doing: the work itself. He takes risks and expands himself, because he doesn't seem focused on 'being successful' or even being admired. In the article he said that, if you're obsessed with your destination, you miss eighty percent of the experience. I've got to remember that: start small; think 'beginning'; enjoy the writing process itself; don't worry about my Oscar yet."

The goal is important. We all need to know what we're working for, even if we change our minds somewhere along the way. But if we don't take satisfaction in some part of the process, we're doomed to be forever dissatisfied. Ed learned, as you will when you open up your daydreams and stories, that one goal can often interfere with the accomplishment of another. In a sense, that's what each of the examples in this chapter has been about— conflicting, mutually exclusive daydreams. For Jennifer, the wish to see herself as not being vengeful interfered with her wish to solve the problem at work. For Andrea, the daydream of never feeling disappointment interfered with her ability to daydream at all—which interfered with her ability to be interested in her work. And for Ed, the wish to be famous, successful, and admired by others interfered with his capacity to do the very writing that these dreams were about.

Although it would be both reductionistic and untrue to say that all problems at work are due to conflicts between your different goals, opening up and exploring some of those conflicts is certainly a worthwhile beginning step to working through job-related difficulties.

Here's an exercise to help you do just that. It probably won't solve the problem, certainly not right away, but it should give you a few good insights into some of the problems you are having and a few potential avenues toward resolution.

EXERCISE:

SOLVING PROBLEMS CREATIVELY

1. Pull out your daydream notebook and open it to a blank page. Note the time and date, and where you are. If you can, also note how you're feeling. Jennifer, for example, was at work, and it was midafternoon. Her head hurt, and her mind felt blank.

2. Write out the difficulty you want to resolve. Keep it brief—two or three sentences at most—but try to capture the essence of the problem. Jennifer wrote two lines describing the difficulty of her work project.

3. Under that description, jot down the next five or six words, phrases, or images that come into your mind. As always, don't worry if they aren't logical or connected to the problem you want to solve. Don't try to get them down in full sentences, either. Just write key words. Jennifer wrote:

Bastard Bob
no direction, no support
wish I was at home
this is stupid
I hate feeling frustrated, helpless, worthless
gaining weight; time for a diet
no good at my job
not true; can't figure this thing out, that's all
my whole body aches
we need to get away from it, come back later

need a massage
take whole group out for drinks tonight; movies too?

Some time after writing this list Jennifer decided to go for a jog before work the next morning. Her back hurt, she was worried about gaining weight, and she needed exercise. Looking back, she also realized that she had needed, as she put it, "to clear my head." But at the time, she had had no idea that her morning run would help solve her problem at work.

You, too, may find that just the process of paying attention to your random thoughts may free you up to take some unexpected—and often apparently unrelated—action. As much as you can, pay attention to the conflicting messages of those thoughts and make sure that you aren't thereby acting out a destructive side of them. For example, going for a jog was a "healthy" move for Jennifer. Going in and telling Bob that she thought he was a bastard would not have been such a good move, although it was an action she considered momentarily.

4. Close your notebook and put it away for a while. This will give you some distance from the daydream and the thoughts that came right after it; and with the distance can come a different perspective, a different point of view—the basis for creative problem-solving.

5. Later—as much as several hours later—go back to the same page. Read the daydream and look at the notes you made. Look for themes that seem to stand out.

Jennifer noticed three basic themes: anger at Bob; anger at herself (expressed in terms of her weight and her inability to do the work); and, finally, a growing sense that she was unfairly blaming herself for something that wasn't her fault, and that she needed to get away from the problem to make herself feel better.

Some of your themes will be familiar feelings; others may surprise you. It can be useful to write these emotions down or to say them out loud—putting them more completely into words that you can see or hear yourself expressing. Another group of themes to look for includes attitudes toward yourself and toward other people. Keep an eye out for assumptions about how you "always" function or how other people "always" are ("always" is a key signal that a thought includes a basic assumption, one of your organizing stories).

Jennifer, as we already know, saw that she wanted to perceive herself as generous, responsive, and understanding—the opposite of vengeful—and at the same time she wanted revenge on Bob. She also had the daydream about rearranging dorm furniture, which juxtaposed the themes of unrecognized revenge and of reorganizing. What themes do you see in your daydreams? Are you resistant, like Andrea? What fears come up for you? What conflicts? Both Andrea and Ed had conflicts about engaging in the here and now, troubles experiencing the process of what they were doing rather than focusing on the ultimate goal. Is that one of your difficulties? How else do you get in your own way? If you can't tell, don't worry. In the next chapters we'll talk about other kinds of interference—and maybe you'll recognize the kinds that keep you yourself from moving on.

CHAPTER SEVEN

Happily Ever After: Daydreams of Love and Romance

DAYDREAMS OF LOVE and romance: someone special, magic moments to treasure forever . . . These fantasies that pervade our culture also color our expectations about adult relationships. Unfortunately, they can lead to disappointment and dissatisfaction when they don't come true as we had imagined. But even more than the expectations they reveal and the hurts they portend, your daydreams about love and romance may tell you more about yourself than any of your other daydreams. How do they do this? And how can such romantic longings help you find real satisfaction in your love life?

You know that many of your daydreams both conceal and reveal your innermost hopes and longings; that they have much more to say than the surface story they tell; and that they can interfere with, and yet also provide a road map to, your desired destination. Your daydreams of romance and love are complex metaphors for many different aspects of your internal world, including your internal conflicts. It may seem too practical, too unromantic to talk about conflicting goals in the realm of love and romance; but watch as we decode some of the hidden material of the daydreams in this chapter, and see how these sparkling jewels of fantasy reveal some of your deepest, most conflicted aims in life. Again, your symbols and your conflicts will probably not correspond exactly to the examples I describe here; but you can apply the basic concepts that unfold as we go along to think about your own personal hopes and struggles, and to use your daydreams to help you move into a more productive place in your own love life.

WHEN DAYDREAMS SHUT DOWN POSSIBILITIES

Mona is a very large woman whose baggy clothes accentuate, rather than hide, her size. When I first met her, she wore no makeup and hid what turned out to be gloriously thick golden hair in a tight bun at the nape of her neck. She described herself as miserably lonely and unhappy, dreaming longingly of "that special man. It's gotten so bad," she told me, "that, each time I meet a man, I immediately start to think about getting married to him. I actually start planning my wedding, imagining how it would be to walk down the aisle toward him. I used to be on the lookout for bells ringing, or the earth shaking—whatever signs you're supposed to get that you've just been hit by Cupid's arrow. I don't even do that anymore. Now I'm satisfied if he doesn't wear a wedding band."

She paused for a moment. "I'm embarrassed that I even think this way. I'm supposed to be a 'liberated woman,' independent, interested in my work, not looking for a man to complete me. But the truth is, I'm tired of being alone. Oh," she went on almost angrily, "you're probably saying to yourself, 'Who would ever be interested in her? No man wants to be with anybody as fat as she is.' " She started to say something else, but I interrupted her.

"You think that's what I think?" I asked.

She scowled at me. "You and everybody else in our society. And don't try to tell me that I'm wrong, because I won't believe you. Look at me. I'm huge. I'm five feet six, and I weigh nearly two hundred pounds. Oh sure, I can be really funny. In fact, everybody at work thinks I'm a gas and a half. People come to me to make them laugh—to make them feel better. But they don't think of dating me; and they'd never imagine falling in love with me."

Then Mona told me one of her organizing stories (although neither she nor I yet knew it). "If I could just lose weight, I'd be happy." When I asked her to elaborate on that daydream, she told me with irritation that it wasn't a daydream: she was *sure* that she would meet a man and have a fulfilling, satisfying relationship if she was thin. "I'd feel better about myself, too, so I wouldn't feel angry or depressed all the time, like I do now. I'd just be content.

"It shouldn't be this way!" she practically shouted. "It really pisses me off that our culture supports men in their prejudice against heavy women, but prejudice does exist. We're not seen as people at all, certainly not as attractive women. . . . You know, just because I'm heavy doesn't mean I'm an ax murderer, but people think that when you're overweight it's because you have more problems than the rest of the world. They think you're weak, that you have no will power. It's like you wear all your issues on your body, and everybody feels they have the right to jump to conclusions, and even to confront you about it. I mean, listen to this: A woman who rides the elevator with me every morning had the gall to tell me that I needed to go on a diet! Oh, it was a classic: 'You have such a pretty face,' she said, 'it's a shame to ruin it.' " Mona's voice was bitter as she imitated the other woman.

For nearly forty-five minutes, Mona talked on without making room for me to say anything, or even to ask a question. At the end of our meeting, I told her that I'd heard a lot of rich material in her daydreams and asked if she would be interested in keeping a daydream journal.

She sighed. "Oh sure," she replied. "I don't have much faith that it'll help, but I've tried everything else. Might as well give it a shot."

But when she returned for our next meeting, she hadn't written a word. "It turns out that I don't have any daydreams," she muttered, looking deeply ashamed.

"Maybe you don't know how to find them," I answered her gently. "Many people don't at first." I suggested that we talk some more, and I would try to help her locate some of her daydreams. As I listened, however, I realized that most of Mona's daydreams were buried under her overarching wish to lose weight. At the same time, they were cut off, sabotaged daily by her compulsive eating behavior. I suggested that, like many other people, she might be using food to stop herself from knowing about herself.

"Why would I do that?" she demanded, sounding more angry than curious. But she sat forward and listened carefully when I explained that the daydreams might contain feelings and thoughts she wasn't comfortable with. When I had finished, she sat back with a sigh. "If you're saying I have to go on a diet to figure out what I'm daydreaming about, we're in trouble. I can't stay on a diet for twenty-five minutes these days."

I proposed that, instead of trying to diet, she try to pay attention to any thoughts she had right before she began to binge-eat. For the time being, she might use her daydream journal simply to note where she was and what she was doing just before she began to think about bingeing. This was a very difficult task for Mona: her eating behavior was like an automatic shutoff valve, closing down all feelings and thoughts about anything except the food. But over time, usually after she had already eaten far more than she "wanted," Mona was able to note the circumstances that occurred just before a binge. And then, one day, halfway through a box of doughnuts, she remembered the daydream that had triggered that particular bout of compulsive eating. Here's how she described it:

"I went back in my mind to the moments before I started stuffing food in my mouth. I realized that I'd been planning this binge for a while—as I do fairly often, I guess. So I went all the way back to the time that I'd started planning it. I'd been at work; I remembered that this guy, Rick, who I've liked for a long time, came over to my desk and started to talk. When I realized that was when it happened, my first thought was, 'Yeah, so what?' And then I recalled the rest of it: my heart started pounding and I started feeling really nervous. I don't know why—the guy was just *talking* to me, for God's sake."

"It's not okay to feel anxious?" I asked quietly.

"I don't know." She looked a little puzzled. "I guess not. Because that *is* when I started thinking about doughnuts . . . where I'd get them, and what kind I'd get. I thought about when I'd buy them, and then I thought about whether I'd eat them in the car on my way home, or if I could wait till I was in my own house and maybe even have a glass of milk with them—at least pretend I'm a normal, civilized human being, you know."

I pointed out to Mona that she was critical not only of her anxious feelings, but also of the way she coped with them: her need for food to calm herself down.

"Well, you would be, too, if you were my size," she replied angrily. "In fact, I imagine you're sitting there thinking what a pig I am, how I can't control myself. . . ." She stopped suddenly. "This is how I felt that day, too. I remember now, I got mad. I thought that Rick was probably looking at me and wondering how I could let myself get so fat. And then I thought, 'He's not so great himself. He's going bald, and he's got a belly.' Maybe I was putting him down because I expected him to reject me—self-protection, you know. But," she went on, slowly, tentatively, "I think there's something else there, too: *I'm* so critical, myself. . . . In fact, maybe that's a big part of what led to the end of my last relationship." She looked hard at me. "I *have* had a relationship, difficult as it may be to believe. His name was Steve. But he never measured up. I didn't like the way he dressed, or the way he wore his hair, or even the kind of work he did."

Mona's food diary gradually became a daydream diary. She began to do the same exercises you have been doing. As she kept track of the random thoughts that followed the daydreams she recorded in her diary, she noticed another important theme.

"You know what?" she asked me. I shook my head no. "It's not just food that keeps my feelings away," she went on. "I use criticism the same way—to shut down and keep people out. Why would I do that? I *think* I want to get close to somebody . . . so why would I push them away?"

This wasn't an easy question to answer, but as Mona continued to jot down some of her daydreams and the thoughts that occurred both before and after them, she gradually started to come up with some explanations. "I guess I can't imagine anybody *I'd* like liking me the way I am; and despite my wish to be thin, I can't seem to change. I'm like that old Groucho Marx joke: I wouldn't belong to any club that would have me for a member. It's not just with men. I do it with women, too. Maybe I'm afraid that people will see not just my physical flaws and flab—well, who can miss that?—but also the ones in my personality. . . ."

Mona worried that other people would be as critical of her as she was of *them*. But as she put it, "that leaves me all alone: I don't let people in, so they won't criticize me, but then I feel lonely and left out and critical of everybody."

I encouraged Mona to use her daydream diary to note instances during the day when she became critical of either herself or someone else, just as she had previously done with her bingeing behavior. Gradually, she became more conscious of the "bind" between her wish to be close, and her critical, angry thoughts, which closed down any possibility of connection. And as she did, she was able to try out some new responses to old situations—first in her daydreams, and later in reality.

"So many times during the day—like when Rick comes by my desk to talk to me—I feel myself get all tense and critical, both of him *and* of me. And then I start to think about eating. But you know what? It's become almost funny. I've come to see that *I'm* the one writing this script. Rick doesn't seem to be judging me the way I'm judging myself—and him."

As a result of this insight, Mona began to notice a new day-dream—one that she had some difficulty allowing to develop. "I wonder if I could let up a little bit on the constant disapproval? It's an appealing idea. . . . But on the other hand, I'm afraid I'd just let myself slack off completely. . . . I'd probably end up weighing seven hundred pounds."

Mona had discovered another crucial factor in her loneliness. Her self-criticism was an attempt to keep herself on the right track, but, like her criticism of others, it kept her from letting any-body in. Similarly, her criticism of others helped protect her from feeling hurt and rejected by them, but it also kept her alone.

As she was struggling with these ideas, Mona had another new experience. She told me, "Rick came up to me again yesterday. And this time I thought to myself, 'You can still have the doughnuts if you want. But give the guy a chance.' I made myself listen to what he had to say, and he was actually *interesting*. And I actually relaxed for a minute!"

Quietly, pensively she went on: "We had a really nice conversation. He didn't ask me out, but, oh, call me crazy, I think that he might. And I'll go if he does. He isn't perfect, and I'm not marrying him tomorrow. But maybe, just maybe, I could let myself have a good time with him."

It wasn't easy for Mona, but now that she recognized that not all the criticism she felt came from outside herself, she was beginning to struggle with the sometimes painful, often surprising implications of the contradiction between her wish to be "perfect" and her wish to be in a real (that is, by definition, imperfect) relationship. Slowly, a little at a time, she began to take chances, to open her imperfect self to less-than-perfect interactions with less-than-perfect people, and as a result she discovered a richer, more complex world of experience waiting for her.

To her surprise and eventual pleasure, Mona's daydreams also underwent another significant shift. First she recognized that she *had* daydreams. And then, after she paid attention to some of them, she found their content changing. For example, although she still wanted to lose weight, she no longer *expected* herself to be "as thin as a model," she said. "It's a nice dream, but it's not my reality." She was beginning to understand that her dream of being thin was a coded version of all her self-criticism: "I'm not good enough as I am." And occasionally she was able to explore other daydreams. "I sometimes imagine that people could like me the way I am. What a relief that is. . . ."

———

In our culture, we tend to place a great value on making dreams come true, *acting* on our dreams, sometimes before we really know what they're telling us. We tend to lose sight of the importance of sitting still, letting our dreams emerge, and exploring them more fully before we do anything about them. But daydreams have so much more to tell us than simply what we should—or even want to—do. Mona's daydream of being thin was intricately tied to her belief that no man would ever care for her as she was. She also learned that her daydream of her wedding day contained the not-so-hidden wish to be loved and loving as she was; but this wish was distorted by her critical thoughts about herself and others, thoughts that kept her shut down and away from the very people she wanted to connect to.

Mona had learned an important lesson: listening carefully to your daydreams doesn't mean never acting, but by acting on one daydream you can sometimes lop off another, closing down your possibilities before you even know they exist.

Besides closing off daydreams, action can also close off feelings: sometimes feelings that are unbearable, confusing, frightening, or otherwise threatening. As we have been seeing, many of our behaviors are attempts to shut off these intolerable feelings. In the process of exploring your daydreams, you will frequently feel confused and doubtful—feelings many of us, like Mona, have difficulty sitting with. But the very fact of tolerating your jumbled, cluttered confusion of emotions will actually move you significantly closer to a genuine understanding of the complex meanings of your daydreams.

This is important: until you can accept "not knowing," you can't find out what you *do* know. As Mona discovered, focusing on her "impossible dream" of perfect thinness left her frustrated and unhappy. It also kept her from having to face her own confusion; but at the same time it interfered with her ability to fulfill—even to know about—other longings.

In the next story, we'll see how stopping, or at least delaying, action long enough to explore the confusing daydreams behind the behavior can lead to valuable self-knowledge—and important changes.

LOOK BEFORE YOU LEAP: WHAT YOUR ACTIONS CAN TELL YOU

Nancy is a vivacious redheaded actress who, as she neared her fortieth birthday, felt "ripped in half" by her love for two men. She came to see me because she felt incapable of making the most difficult and crucial decision in her life.

"David, my husband, was the most glamorous, exciting, devastatingly handsome man I had ever known," she told me. "He asked me to marry him exactly one month after we met, and I said 'Yes!' immediately. He seemed to love everything about me—even the fact that I was scatterbrained and disorganized. He told me that he admired me for pursuing my acting career, which was so important to me—even though it left me with a crazy schedule and a chaotic life.

"Maybe I should have listened to my friends. They didn't like David from the beginning. It seemed they saw something a little forced, maybe artificial, about him. They said I should take some time to get to know him before jumping into marriage. But I put it down to sour grapes—to envy of me for being so lucky to have found this wonderful man who adored me as much as I adored him.

"Shortly after we married, I found out that David had quite a temper. I would do something he didn't like and he would blow up at me. At first I accepted it. At least he was passionate. I'd been with a 'nice guy' for two years before I met David, and he'd gotten so boring and predictable that he made my skin crawl. David, on the other hand, was exciting. To tell you the truth, I think I loved the drama of our life together. We would have these wild fights where we were shouting and screaming, sometimes throwing things. There were a few times that I was afraid he would hit me; and once or twice he grabbed me and shook me so hard I thought my neck would break. But the worst times were when he said terrible, cruel things. He would break my heart. Sometimes I would burst into tears, run upstairs, and lock the bedroom door; and he would come after me, bang on the door, threaten to tear it down. But in those early days, we would always end up in each other's arms, usually both sobbing; he would apologize and tell me how much he loved me; we would have wonderful sex, and end up feeling closer to each other than ever.

"But then, after we'd been together about six years, I wanted to start a family. At first he just put me off. Then he told me I was too scatterbrained to have children. That really hurt. What had happened to the man who said he loved me the way I was? We had some terrible arguments about it. And then arguments over other things—my housekeeping skills, his stinginess—got worse. Sex and romance went out the window. When we did sleep together, which was not very often, it was no more than an old-fashioned 'wham bam, thank you, ma'am.'

"Then—I don't know how, since I was feeling so low—I landed a job on a soap opera. Not a big or a glamorous part, but it was a real acting job—and I got paid! David seemed proud of me, and things got better between us. We had a couple of nice, intimate evenings together. We started to have sex again, although there was no discussion of trying to have a child. Our life began to get a little better. But I guess it wasn't enough. I still longed for the David who *adored* me. Then, recently, I met Alex, who works on the show. Alex thinks I'm gorgeous, brilliant, and a fabulous actress. He brings me little gifts every day. He's just the sweetest, nicest, most loving man I've ever met. I told myself that we were just friends, but then he wanted to take me out after my sixth month on the show—to celebrate! David was busy. I went. And . . . we started an affair. And now I'm in a terrible bind. I still love David—but I also love Alex. I want to be with both of them."

Nancy's daydreams were of impossible resolutions to her "bind." She wanted to be with David, if only he could be more like Alex. And she wanted to be with Alex, if only it would not mean leaving David. These wishes reflected her strongly clashing emotions, but they did not help clarify her situation or direct her toward any realistic decisions. Unlike Andrea, who shut down her daydreams in order not to repeat the painful disappointment she remembered from childhood, Nancy *knew* that she daydreamed—in fact, Nancy had an overwhelming number of fantasies. But this flood of daydreams served the same purpose as Andrea's absence of imagery: they kept her from knowing something about herself. Like Andrea, Nancy had difficulty playing with her daydreams: they either happened or they didn't happen. She felt that she had no control over them.

"Playing" may seem to be a strange word for exploring the contradictory and often painful feelings both Nancy and Andrea struggled with. But, taken in its broadest sense, it's an extremely useful concept in the work we are doing. "Playing" is the way children learn about themselves and the world in which they live. It is no coincidence that it is also the term chosen by the British pediatrician and psychologist D. W. Winnicott to describe what we do when we examine our internal fantasy world. Like many of the games of childhood, this "playing" is a crucial component of the journey to self-knowledge and true self-expression, and it's what I asked Nancy to do now: take some time to contemplate these personal reveries, so that she might better understand what she was trying to tell herself *before* she acted. As she learned to stop and sift through her thoughts, Nancy did indeed start to confront aspects of herself she had previously not examined.

For example, one day she told me, "The other day, David and I were talking about O. J. Simpson, and we started discussing whether it was ever okay to kill another person. And he said that he thought it was okay for a man to kill his wife if she was sleeping around on him." Nancy's eyes filled with tears. "I didn't know what to think. Does that mean that David would kill me if he found out that I was having an affair?"

I asked Nancy to tell me what she imagined. Still tearful, she replied, "I think he was threatening me. I don't think he knows about Alex, but maybe he senses something. And . . . I don't know . . . I guess I can imagine him killing me. He'd feel horrible about it afterwards, I'm sure; but it'd be too late."

This was not a daydream I was willing to take lightly. At the same time, it was crucial that we not immediately jump to the conclusion that David actually would become—was even capable of being—a murderer. Nancy's daydream might have represented unconscious knowledge about David, but it might also have reflected her unrecognized feelings about his verbal abusiveness— something she tended to minimize or disregard. Furthermore, it might have contained information about other dynamics in the relationship, feelings and thoughts that were not immediately accessible to Nancy.

It is sometimes extremely difficult to assess the actual risk of a relationship on your own; if you have any suspicion that your partner may become physically abusive, it is always important to seek outside, professional assistance to figure out just what you are trying to tell yourself and to determine whether or not you are in danger. But sometimes, giving yourself permission to explore your daydreams and to follow your free associations can help illuminate your situation.

Since Nancy insisted that David's verbal aggression was

insignificant, we focused specifically on the question of his past violence and the intricacies of their current relationship. "I know I tend to dramatize everything," Nancy finally concluded. "I mean, David never did more than shake me up a little. I know that wasn't good, but he didn't abuse me. And he hasn't done anything remotely physical in years. In fact, when he gets really angry now, he walks out. I don't think he'll hurt me."

Unlike some women in physically abusive relationships, Nancy did not think that she deserved to be hurt, nor did she seem to be denying the severity of David's reactions and behavior, past or present. But there were other meanings embedded in her fantasies and her wish to remain with David despite what she sometimes saw as his "potential for violence." To get to this information, I asked Nancy to push a little further into her daydream about what would happen if David found out that she was having an affair.

"Well, I'm pretty sure he has no idea that I'm having an affair," Nancy said, "although I imagine he may have some sense of it unconsciously. And I guess one daydream is that he was threatening me, without realizing what he was doing, because he *does* unconsciously suspect. . . . But—this is a *disturbed* thought—I guess it's what you mean by going further with my daydream, but I hate to believe I could even think this. . . ." She took a deep breath, then continued. "I seem to be getting a sick kind of pleasure out of imagining David getting violent."

Like Andrea's refusal to allow herself to daydream, and like Mona's binges, Nancy's criticism of her daydream as "sick" was a way of trying to keep back some of the feelings and thoughts she was afraid to face. This resistance is, as I have said before, normal. It is one of the ways we adapt to conflict, both internal and external. However, this self-criticism interferes with our ability to explore daydreams, and thereby to understand ourselves more fully. The lack of self-knowledge that results keeps us in turn from making the changes we most want to make.

I wondered how Nancy would understand these daydream thoughts if she did not call them "sick." "Can you think of any nonjudgmental words to describe the same feelings?"

After a few moments' thought, she said, "Well, I guess I'd say I'm conflicted—although that feels like an understatement. And . . ." She looked surprised at her own thought. "Maybe thinking that David would try to kill me is a way of solving the conflict. Because if he got violent I wouldn't have a choice, I'd *have* to leave. I mean, I wouldn't stand for him shaking me up the way he used to anymore. . . ."

Over the next weeks, Nancy kept track of her daydreams about David's potential violence. She paid close attention to what was happening immediately before she noticed each daydream, and she also noted her first thoughts after each one. One issue that kept coming up was what she called " 'the baby problem.' I'm almost forty years old, for God's sake. I don't want to end up staying with David and waking up in a year and realizing it's too late to meet another man and start a family with *him*. But I'm not sure that Alex is the solution, either. . . . I mean, I have daydreams about being with him, even having his baby, but I don't know if I want to marry him. Sometimes I imagine having a baby, not knowing whose it is; or staying friends with both Alex and David but not living with either one of them. And sometimes I imagine leaving them both. Maybe I'd go to live with my parents. They'd take care of me; but I'd go crazy in a few days. Maybe I could rent a small studio apartment and live by myself. I'd get a cat or a dog—maybe one of each." Her thoughts and words tumbled on. "But if the show ends, or I lose my part in it, I'd be in trouble; I wouldn't want Alex to support me, and David won't give me a penny for alimony."

As she continued to track these daydreams, her subsequent thoughts led Nancy to other previously unrecognized perceptions. "Sometimes I imagine David coming to me, really apologetic, and telling me that he's met someone else." She was silent, but there were tears in her eyes. "Just thinking about that really hurts me. But then . . . there's another thought that comes right after. I have another—secret—daydream. I usually stop myself from thinking it 'out loud'—in my own head. And then I forget it. Talk about sick. . . ." She hesitated, then seemed to push herself to say the rest. "It's another part of the 'getting pleasure out of imagining David hitting me' daydream: I think I really *long* for David to get violent. *Whew.* I said it. . . . I've been letting myself think about it recently. When I look at the words I write in my notebook after it, it seems pretty obvious what it means. I think I would see his violence as a real indication of how much he loved me. And *that's* what I really want—to know that he loves me, cares about me, needs me."

Nancy's daydreams were not signally that she wanted David to be violent in reality. By following her daydream thoughts, however, she cracked open the door to this previously unrecognized connection. Her life didn't suddenly change; but that tiny opening shifted her self-awareness and gradually led to a profoundly new perspective—and widely expanded possibilities.

Understanding some of the complex meanings of her daydream images did not enable Nancy to break instantly out of the painful bind of loving two men. But over time she realized that Alex reminded her of the "nice guy" she had dated for two years before she married David. "He doesn't make my skin crawl . . . yet," she said. "But I guess I like the passion and excitement of my old relationship with David. I just wonder if we could have it without so much hostility; and without my feeling like I'm in danger—either physically or psychologically. I don't know how we can resolve the baby thing, but we have to start with the question of whether or not there's still some passion and real compatibility between us, and then whether or not we might rekindle it in a new way."

Dr. Stephen Mitchell, a New York City psychologist and author, tells us that Nancy's struggle is a common one: conflicts in love are often attempts to mediate between passion on one side and security on the other. For Nancy, stability without some risk and excitement was, ultimately, boring. Although all her behavior had multiple meanings, she now realized that one of the points of her affair with Alex, and perhaps even of her wish for a baby, was an unrecognized wish to spice up her relationship with David.

Perhaps you find passion in the deepened bond of a more mellow but more secure relationship; or maybe you repeatedly end old relationships and start up new ones because the throes of early passion make you feel more alive than the security of a long-term relationship. Or perhaps you yearn to find a way to integrate the two, to experience passion in a long-term, secure relationship. Whatever the case, your daydreams can hold clues to your own preferences, the conflicts that accompany them, and the possibilities for change; but remember that there is no "correct answer" here. The longings, satisfactions, and conflicts in your love life are highly complex. To find the solution that works for you requires self-knowledge and acceptance, not self-criticism and externally imposed values. Self-knowledge comes slowly. You need to be patient with your blocks: they're adaptive defenses you have developed to help you cope with overwhelming or disturbing feelings, confusing wishes, and conflicting needs.

In the next story, you'll see how "unacceptable" daydreams actually held the keys to one man's fears of commitment. As you read on, think about your own inadmissible daydreams, and try to follow the themes they contain without making value judgments about their content.

THE INELIGIBLE BACHELOR:
DAYDREAMS AND COMMITMENT

The first thing I noticed when I met Larry was how handsome he was. The next was that he was incredibly charming. He seemed to know these things about himself, but, as he put it, "That's part of the problem. I get invited to every party thrown by my friends and acquaintances; I'm always being fixed up on dates with beautiful, interesting women; and I don't have any difficulty picking up women on my own, either. I'm thirty-five years old and the town's most eligible bachelor.

"I know it doesn't sound like much of a problem, but it really is. I'd like to settle down; I want to have a family. But I can't seem to do it. I mean, right now I'm involved with a wonderful woman. She's beautiful, thoughtful, smart. She's ten years older than I am, but that doesn't bother me, though it makes her a little uncomfortable sometimes. We talk about it—we have a really open, wonderful relationship that way. The problem is that I dream of being madly in love with a woman, not being able to stand being away from her for a minute, adoring everything about her. And that's not what I feel about Joanna. I really love her. We talk about getting married, having kids, or, if she can't have them naturally, adopting. I *want* to marry her. But that overwhelming passion isn't there.

"I've got to make a decision. I can't keep leading her on like this. It's not fair to her. She wants to settle down herself, and if I'm not going to do it, she needs to be free to meet someone else. I'm not ready to make a permanent commitment to her . . . but I can't stand thinking about not being with her anymore.

"Thing is, when I'm away from her, I miss her so much. But then, when we're together . . . well, for the first few hours I'm thrilled to be with her, and then I start to see all of her flaws, her failings, the things I don't like so much about her.

"It's the same thing with sex. When Joanna walks into a room, every man's head turns to look at her, she's so hot. I get turned on as soon as I see her. But then I start to notice that her makeup's smudged; or she has a pimple on her face; or I don't like the outfit she's wearing. I see another good-looking woman and I start to imagine going to bed with *her*. Like the other day, we were out at our favorite restaurant and there were two gorgeous women at a table near us. I couldn't believe myself. I started thinking about having sex with the two of them together."

I asked Larry if he could tell me more about this daydream. "Well, I don't like to think about it. My dad cheated on my mom for years. My mom was really, really hurt. I hate to think I might be like him. It's one of the reasons I don't settle down. It wouldn't be fair to the woman."

"Do you think thinking about something is the same thing as acting on it?" I asked him.

"Well, no, not when you put it that way. Although maybe I do, at least a little bit, since I do feel guilty when I start to have these kinds of thoughts." After a few moments he added, "But if I can't think about my thoughts, what can I think about? I feel kind of uncomfortable telling you about them—even more than thinking about them." He grinned boyishly. "This is some job you've got—listening to other people's sexual fantasies."

As we laughed together, some of the tension broke, and Larry felt ready to begin the process of exploring these extremely private, often embarrassing vehicles of information about his most intimate self: his sexual daydreams. Sexual and romantic daydreams are often linked in a variety of interesting ways—some obvious and some not. Yet romantic daydreams are generally far easier to talk about than sexual ones. Freud believed that this was because conflicts about unacceptable sexual and aggressive wishes were at the bottom of all neurotic difficulties. However, Heinz Kohut, a psychoanalyst who broke from Freudian tradition in the 1970s, concluded that it's often the other way around: sexual material is actually symbolic of other conflicts. In other words, we are inhibited from exploring sexual daydreams not only because of social taboos, but also because they often contain vivid representations of other unacceptable or conflict-ridden feelings and thoughts about ourselves and other people, images that we have never processed because they are inadmissible even to our inner-most selves.

Thinking about his daydreams this way made it easier for Larry to talk about the brief thoughts he had had when he looked at the two woman in the restaurant. "I imagined what it would be like to be in bed with these two gorgeous women; one would be kissing and fondling me, the other kissing and fondling *her*. Then I imagined them both doing things to me, me lying there passively, letting them 'have their way with me.' Don't get me wrong. Sex with Joanna is out of this world. And we're able to share the action. I mean, I'm not usually passive sexually, but sometimes I like for a woman to take over the more aggressive role so I can lie back and receive some of the time. And Joanna's cool with that, although she also loves it when I'm the aggressor. I mean, sex with her is dynamite. I don't understand why I'm not satisfied with it."

I asked Larry to associate to the image of "lying back and receiving."

His eyes darkened. "Well, to tell you the truth, there's more to that daydream. I feel really uncomfortable talking about it. But since I've gone this far . . ." He took a deep breath. "I actually imagine being tied down by the women. They play me like an instrument, fondling me, kissing me, getting me more and more excited, but not letting me come, till I think I can't stand it. Then one of them sits on my dick and the other one kisses me on the mouth, and I come. And it's heaven."

Although Larry was embarrassed, he was interested when I asked him if he could tell me what themes he saw in the daydream.

"Well, there's the 'lying back and receiving' themes you asked me about. . . ." Larry had learned to note his next thoughts as he analyzed a daydream. So he immediately said, "My associa-tion to *that* theme was 'being tied down'! Which is what I'm always feeling with Joanna. Am I saying that I can only receive if I'm tied down?"

Larry had articulated his own conflict: his longing to have someone else take control, and his fear of the very same thing. "You know, I had a sort of half-thought about this the other day. I mean, it occurred to me that maybe I'm with an older woman because I feel like I *could* let her take over once in a while, that I don't always have to be the 'man.' But I see now that that also scared me to death."

I suggested that Larry try to notice the next time he began to daydream about other women. "See if you can go back in your head to the moments right before you start to have the fantasy: what you're doing, thinking, feeling, saying; who you're with. There may be some important clues to your conflicts in those thoughts."

The next time we met, Larry was eager to talk about his daydreams. "It's so interesting," he told me excitedly, pushing his dark hair out of his eyes. "I was with Joanna. We were curled up together on the couch, watching TV. I was having a beer. A commercial came on, a gorgeous blonde in a bathing suit—I don't even remember what it was an ad for. And I immediately started to think about what that woman would be like in bed. I had a quick flash of what it would be like with her and another woman, the two of them fucking my brains out; and then I tried to back up, to figure out what I'd been thinking about right before. All I could come up with was that I'd been feeling really cozy, comfortable, loving. Joanna had just brought me the beer and had curled up beside me. I'd noticed that she had a pimple on her nose. And that's when the blonde came on.

"But I kept trying to remember exactly what else was going on. And as I thought about how cozy Jo and I had been, I recalled another thought I'd had—either as the commercial started or just before it. But anyway, before I started to have the daydream, I had the thought that it was dangerous to feel so comfortable. I've had that thought plenty of times, but I've never put it together with the daydream before."

I asked him what he made of that thought.

"Well, I've always worried about being too dependent on one person. Maybe it's why I like to imagine having sex with two women—it's my version of safe sex, like not putting all your eggs in one basket. If one of them messes up, doesn't satisfy me, lets me down somehow, I'll still be okay, because there's always the other one."

"What about the image of them 'fucking your brains out'?" I asked.

He laughed. "Then I couldn't think; I couldn't worry. I'd just have to go with the flow." He paused for a minute. "Listen to me," he went on. "I guess I *am* always afraid of being let down by someone I supposedly trust. Maybe that's why I'm always looking for Joanna's flaws—so I can be prepared for the ways she's going to let me down. Well, I have plenty of experience with that—my dad certainly let my mother down, hurt her real bad; and I guess he hurt me, too, by being such a bad role model, and somebody I couldn't really count on, either. I always said I was going to be the opposite of him, but it looks like I'm like him more than I realized. I can't make a commitment to one person any more than he could."

I asked if Larry thought his father was also afraid of being hurt by someone he committed himself to. He was silent for a moment, then said, "You know, I've never wanted to feel any sympathy for him. But as soon as you said that, I started to think that maybe he wanted to be taken care of, like me, but was afraid of it, too. And I had this flash of a thought—let's see if I can even put it into words—I guess it was sort of about being afraid of losing himself in the other person. I mean, if you really let go, give yourself over to another person, can you come back out of it? It's like you melt into them, and then, I guess I wonder, can you get solid again? I don't have any idea if that was my dad's fear; but it sure is mine!"

Larry had opened up the door to powerful images and striking contrasts in his psyche. His romantic and sexual daydreams contained crucial keys to his longing for and fears of being dependent on someone else. He was beginning to understand that his fear of commitment was directly related to his anxiety about his own unknown wish to give up control, to let someone else take over, because he was also afraid that, once having done this, he would never recover his own separate self.

Uncovering these conflicts did not suddenly make Larry able to commit himself to his relationship with Joanna, but at least now he knew what some of the demons were. When he became disillusioned with Joanna or began to daydream about another woman, he was able to backtrack in his own mind to find the trigger to the feelings; and now that he knew what to look for, he wasn't surprised to find that many times it was a reaction to feeling close to her. For Larry, that close feeling seemed to open up a longing to become so dependent that he felt his sense of his own identity disappear. Both his daydreams of being with other women and his criticism of Joanna shored up Larry's sense of his separate self, but they also interfered with his ability to fulfill his wish to be completely involved with the woman he loved. Recognizing the conflicts for what they were, Larry was able to tolerate his confusion instead of feeling that he had to "do something about it." As he put it, "I know I love Joanna. I know I'm afraid of loving her. But we've been talking about it; and she's okay with where I am at. If she can live with it, I can live with it. And actually, now that it's out in the open, I'm not feeling quite so pressured . . . at least for the moment."

LOVE, SEX, AND INTIMACY: MAKING CONNECTIONS

Psychologists have long recognized that we human beings crave intimacy with others. It is part of our makeup. But along with a wish for closeness can go a fear of loss of independence: a wish for and a fear of melding with another person that, as Larry put it, could potentially leave us without a sense of our individuality. This struggle to find a comfortable balance between connectedness to and separateness from important others is a basic factor in how we feel about both ourselves and the people who populate our world.

How does this connect to your romantic and sexual daydreams? If you think about it, what is more intimate than romance and sex? We play out our anxieties and wishes about intimacy, our wishes for and fears of both closeness and separateness, in the theater of our sexual and romantic imaginings, as well as in our relationships themselves.

Here's an exercise that will help you, as you begin to examine your daydreams about love and romance and, yes, sex, to understand something of your own conflicts, anxieties, fears and longings about closeness, love, and intimacy with another human being.

EXERCISE:

LOVE AND . . .
JUST WHAT DO YOU
REALLY WANT?

1. Pull out a pen and your daydream notebook, but don't open it yet. Before you write anything, close your eyes and think about your favorite romantic movie, play, or novel: whether it's a

classic like *Pride and Prejudice* or *Wuthering Heights* or a contemporary romance by Danielle Steele, let yourself steep in the imagery, the story, the parts that you love.

2. Now open your notebook to a blank page and write down the next few thoughts that come into your mind. They don't have to be about the story, and they don't have to be full sentences or even phrases.

Mona's favorite, for example, was the movie *Sleepless in Seattle*. Her list looked like this:

Sweet
Feminine
Independent
Loving, vulnerable
Funny
Want to love
Afraid

3. Look over the list and choose one word or phrase that you would like to think about, and one that you would like to discard.

4. Now ask yourself the following questions about *each* of these two phrases:

- What comes to my mine when I think of this phrase?
- What feeling does it bring up in me?
- What connections do I automatically make to these feelings? Why?
- Can I think of at least one alternative view of these situations?

It's always a good idea to write your answers down in order to establish them more solidly in your mind's eye. But whether you write them or not, don't stop with what you already know. Push the envelope. Let yourself expand on your romantic fantasies. Find what else is there inside you, waiting for you to recognize it.

Mona, for example, chose the words "sweet" and "feminine" to think about. Here's what she said: "I've always imagined my sweet little 'feminine' Meg Ryan self locked away inside my big fat self; and I guess I've believed some man had the key to find it. But I'm starting to see that being feminine really has nothing to do with size *or* sweetness. It's all about self-image. I'm a woman; that makes me feminine by definition. And once I started acting like I knew that, I started feeling different. And, amazingly, people started responding differently to me. I mean, I feel friendlier, so I smile at men . . . and they smile back! And then I feel even better about myself, so I start to talk to someone. . . . And they seem more than happy to talk to me!"

Don't stop with these thoughts about a movie or book. You can learn a tremendous amount about your organizing stories, your assumptions about yourself and other people, through your romantic daydreams. Pay attention to any details that stand out for any reason; and pay equally close attention to those you want to ignore. Write down some of these ideas; then ask yourself the questions listed above. As you try to answer them, you will find yourself following the threads of those details to the stories they hide. Though some of them will seem familiar, others will reveal some surprising data on yourself and your deepest conflicts about closeness. Like Mona and Larry, you may find that you use your daydreams of perfect love to keep intimacy at a manageable level: that your dreams of "happily ever after" disguise deep conflicts about closeness, autonomy, even fantasies of merging with another. You may close off feelings that you associate with the opposite sex; or, like Nancy, you may learn something about your need for excitement or stability, and some of your conflicts over that need. And you may learn something new about your expectations (or lack thereof) for other people, and ways that you protect yourself from potential disappointment and hurt.

Whatever you discover, whatever your personal conflicts over intimacy, remember that it is *completely natural* to have them. Exploring your daydreams will not end your personal struggles to find the degree of connectedness and separateness that works for you. What these expeditions into your internal world can do is to offer you a clearer understanding of yourself—your fears and longings, your assumptions and automatic defenses—so that you can move more easily, and more safely, through both the white waters of romantic passion and the still but deep waters of quiet commitment.

CHAPTER EIGHT

The Addams Family Versus the Brady Bunch (or: The Hospital Gave Me to the Wrong Parents!)

LIKE MOST CHILDREN, my six-year-old son knows every possible ploy to get me to bend to his will. In the grocery store, when he wants to buy fourteen boxes of sugar-coated, artificially colored (and flavored) cereals; in the play-ground, when he wants to shoot his Super Soaker at the obnoxious little girl who won't give up her swing ("Just one time, Mommy"); or in the toy store, where he wants one of everything—in each of these and a million other places, he will try his best to win me over to his point of view. Sometimes he pleads. Sometimes he tries bargaining: "I'll clean my room *forever* if you'll just let me . . ." Other times he tries to convince me that every other kid he knows has whatever it is that he says he needs so badly, and that if he doesn't get it he'll be laughed out of the union of six-year-old boys. And, of course, sometimes he turns on the charm, sweetly informing me that I'm just the *best* mom, and it would be so nice if I would let him . . .

But sometimes, when his techniques don't work and I manage to stand firm, he just loses it. Flushed and furious, he'll yell, "You're not the best mom—you're the meanest mom in the world! I'm going to run away and find a *better* family!"

Painful as it is to be informed by our children that we're the worst, meanest, most unfair parents who ever lived, we all remember times from our own childhood when we felt exactly the same way about our own moms and dads—or brothers and sisters, grandparents, uncles, aunts, or cousins. Even if you don't have any of these memories, you—like all children—probably aimed some of your most frightening and confusing feelings in a safer direction: scary stories about evil stepmothers who wanted to murder innocent children, and magical creatures who rescued them just in time. Remember when you saw Dorothy throw that pail of water on the Wicked Witch of the West in *The Wizard of Oz*—making her (finally!) melt away? Weren't there a few secret times when you wondered if that bucket trick might work on someone else, maybe somebody in your *own* house who kept saying no to *your* requests?

From the time we're very little (and even though we may not always be conscious of it), most of us have at least two conflicting families playing tug of war in our imaginations: the flawed, sometimes happy, often difficult, and even hurtful one of "reality," and the loving and joyously conflict-free one (perhaps modeled on any number of happy TV sitcom households) of our daydreams. Of course, these inner battles between that ideal, wonderful family we wish we'd had and the often disappointing folks we actually grew up with don't stop with childhood.

One of the adaptive tasks of daydreams all through life is to help us make peace with the contrast between these different families. But sometimes the conflicts are not so easy to resolve. Though you may have successfully pushed them out of your conscious thoughts, you are still responding to them, motivated by them as much as you were when you first daydreamed about what it would take to make (choose one) Mommy, Grandpa, Aunt Mildred, Daddy, or bratty Cousin Billy melt into the kitchen floor. These internal (and sometimes external) tugs of war color not only your perceptions of yourself and your family, but also your entire world of relationships.

We've seen some of the subtle and ingenious ways in which daydreams help us adapt to reality and reconcile our inner and outer lives. Our psyches continually strive to make sense of each new circumstance, person, or experience we face, and—as you now know—daydreams are important tools in the construction of that sense. Daydreams about family—both past and present, wished-for and actual—are filled with meaning; for precisely this reason, they can be particularly difficult to decode. For example, you may be sure that you had a happy, carefree childhood; but as you journey through your daydreams, you will discover some mixed, even unpleasant feelings about that wonderful time. On the other hand, if what you recall of your childhood is one miserable, unhappy experience after another, your daydreams will unquestionably reveal (although not necessarily right away) some hidden happy feelings as well.

This discovery of mixed emotions will occur for one simple

reason: no one escapes conflict growing up, dealing with his or her family. From our earliest experiences, love exists along with hate; happiness along with sadness, longing, and the pain of loss; and secret, stolen, guilty pleasures along with a sense of security and satisfaction. Remember: the existence of these conflicts doesn't mean that your parents were as cruel and rotten as you may sometimes have felt—simply that they, like you, were (and are) human. But because not all of these clashing emotions are acceptable, either to ourselves or to the important people we must get along with both as children and as adults, we don't always process them very well. They end up as a bewildering morass of half-conscious memories and feelings, of daydreams that seem to represent one thing but when explored more thoroughly reveal something else altogether.

Why make the effort to untangle all these threads, to sort through these confusing (and not always pleasant) emotions? Because your unrecognized conflicts about your family, your unquestioned but warring assumptions and beliefs, can produce some of the biggest obstacles you face today. These daydreams color and reinforce your perceptions of yourself and others not only in your family of origin, but also in your entire world of relationships—at work, with friends, with your spouse, lover, and children, with casual acquaintances, people you've just met, and people you want to meet.

As you begin to open up this area of your daydream world, you may have to work a little harder to let go, to follow and make sense of some of your random, disorganized, and disconnected thoughts. But if you stick with it, allow your mind to wander and make whatever connections it will, no matter how silly, surprising, or unnerving those connections might seem at first, you will come upon some basic information about yourself and how you live your life.

While you are sifting through the batch of daydreams in this chapter, and when you begin working on your own images, thoughts, and associations, try to be especially patient with yourself. And save some patience for your family as well. Remember not to take your daydreams literally. In the realm of daydreams, what you see is not necessarily what you got. Play with your thoughts, your feelings, your connections, your mental pictures, and your recollections.

Some old patterns are so reflexive that we automatically fall into them before we have a clue that there is a daydream involved. We just find ourselves running around the same old pitted track, ending up at the same dead ends. Even when we make a conscious decision not to be like our parents, we can unwittingly end up repeating old patterns that we don't know exist. But you *can* learn to stop yourself before you make these habitual swerves into familiar places.

You're now going to meet a few people who have managed to do that for themselves—who have explored their daydreams about their families and discovered some of the meanings of the stories they tell themselves. Through this internal work, they've found some of the potholes that keep tripping them up. As you read their stories, look for clues about how you, too, might be able to see the family ruts in your own path, and how you might pave some new, smoother roads to happier and more effective solutions (other than throwing a bucket of water at a witch).

DADDY'S GIRL: FAMILY ISSUES THAT RESURFACE IN THE NEXT GENERATION

Dan was a tall, thin man whose blue-black hair contrasted powerfully with his almost ghostly-pale complexion. He was not happy about being in my office.

"This is all my wife's idea," he snapped at me. "I don't need or want to be here. I'm not the one who has the problems. Now, my daughter Julie, on the other hand—well, she *is* the problem. *She* should be seeing someone, not me. I told Stacy, my wife, that it's a waste of time and money, my coming here. There's nothing you can do . . . nothing anyone could do."

I listened carefully. The fact that Dan *had* come to see me indicated some hope, perhaps hidden even from himself—some daydream about the future that he hadn't yet acknowledged.

He continued angrily. "That girl's a bad seed: a mean-natured, self-centered little bitch. She has an impossible mouth—arguing, complaining, never taking no for an answer. And heaven help us if we ask her to help out around the house. She doesn't lift a finger. . . . If I'd been like my own father, I'd have beaten it out of her by now. Especially when she puts on her Queen of England act, like she's so much better than all the rest of us. But I refuse to sink that low, even if it would be the best thing for all of us.

"I wish to God *you* could do something. But the very fact that I'm the one who's here is just one more sign of how our family has everything ass-backwards. *She* should be here, not me. But, no, life in our house revolves around Queen Julie. Sweet Jesus—she even invades my work life!"

I asked how that happened.

"Sometimes I find myself worrying about what she's up to . . . and that's the end of my concentration. She distracts me completely from whatever I'm doing."

I asked if he could think of any specific examples of these daydreams about Julie that interrupted his work.

"I can give you a hundred, probably more. But here's one. It happened yesterday, in fact. I was in a goddamned meeting, and all of a sudden I remembered our last conversation. I had told her I was going to cut off her allowance if she didn't straighten out, and she blew up at me, screaming about how unfair I am. When I told her she couldn't talk to me that way, she walked out of the house, slamming the door behind her.

"I just didn't know what to do. Maybe I *should* have slapped her. I never have been good at punishing her. My wife says I wasn't ever strict enough with her. . . . She's always complained that Julie could wrap me around her little finger. She was a real 'daddy's girl.' Stubborn, it was true. Just like her grandfather. But what a kid—a top-notch athlete, an A student, and cute as a button to boot. Spoiled rotten . . ." He stopped for a moment. "Maybe that part *is* my fault; but, you know, I'm really tired of taking all the blame. Maybe it's just in her genes. She's like her grandfather—my father—in more ways than I ever realized. He was a real bastard. Maybe she's just inherited his personality."

He took a deep breath. "You asked me a question. . . . Oh yeah, how does she interfere with my work? Well, like I said, I was in a meeting yesterday—a boring, unnecessary meeting that my bosses, bless them, somehow see as more important than the work I'm actually *supposed* to be doing—although if I don't do *that* work, you can bet I'll hear about it. Truth is, they'd really be happy if I worked ninety hours a week; the eighty-five hours I already work aren't enough for them.

"So I had to go and listen to some young wet-behind-the ears little creep with a brand-new M.B.A. go on for two hours about a subject I know inside out. It was an insult—not just to me, but to all of us older, more experienced guys."

I sympathized with the difficulty of this position.

He went on: "One of the things my dad believed in is that you always treat your elders with respect—whatever you really feel. I wish I had some of that from these young M.B.A.'s Of course, the respect I showed my father never meant anything except that I grew up afraid of his belt or the back of his hand. The thing is, I didn't want to have that kind of a phony relationship with Julie." He stopped and looked at me. "Damn! You see what I mean. Here she is again, creeping into every conversation, every thought."

I reminded Dan that Julie wasn't in the room with us, and I suggested that her appearance in his thoughts meant something not just about her but also about him. We could discover just what it meant by following his train of thoughts.

"And will that solve my problems with Julie?" he demanded. I told him I couldn't promise that it would solve them but I would guarantee he would learn something important—and useful—about himself, and most probably about his relationship with Julie as well.

"Okay," he sighed. "Well, my thoughts go back to that god-damned meeting. *There's* a place where I feel like I don't get any respect. In fact, Stacy's always on me to stand up for myself at work. I never get the recognition I . . ." He broke off. "Wait a minute. Are you saying there might be a connection between my feeling that Julie doesn't respect me and the way my bosses treat me? Like . . . that they don't respect me, either?" I pointed out that I wasn't saying anything, that this was his thought—and that it seemed quite significant. He gazed pensively into space for a few moments. "Well, I can go even one better here. It's how I've always felt about my dad, too—that he had no respect for me. But, okay—so what does this mean?"

Dan had made an extremely important connection between his feelings about his daughter, his father, and his bosses. But he was right: that connection itself was not enough. The next step was to discover what these feelings meant about *him*—in Dan's case, how he viewed himself and how that self-view affected his interactions with the people he cared about most.

To discover more about these perceptions, I encouraged him to pay attention to whatever daydreams unfolded over the next few days, wherever and whenever they occurred, even if they seemed to be interfering with his work. He was still doubtful that this process was more than a waste of time, but, as he put it, "I'm desperate. I'm ready to try anything."

In fact, he was fascinated by what he found. "Yesterday," he told me when we met next, "I was sitting at my desk doing my work when I suddenly realized that Julie had slipped into my head. I started to get angry, like I always do, that she was interrupting my work, but then I thought about what you said. So I tried to go back to what I was thinking about before she 'came into' my head. It wasn't that hard to figure out, actually. I was doing some work I hate—number crunching, which drives me crazy—and I had this thought that Julie ought to be grateful to me for busting my ass doing a job I hate so that I can support her in the manner to which she wants to stay accustomed. And, of course, that brought me back to the thought about how ungrateful she actually is. And—as always—how disrespectful.

"And later, when I got pissed at her again, I realized it was right after my boss gave me a hard time about some work that someone else had done wrong. And I realized that, just before I got pissed at Julie, I had the flash of a thought—get this!—that 'Julie would never put up with anybody talking to her like this!' " He was silent for a moment. When he spoke again, it was to put into words something he had long known but never articulated, even to himself. "I've always admired Julie for her spunk. Truth is, I *wish* I could have stood up to my father the way she stands up to me. He would have murdered me, but I would have felt so much better about myself."

This time the silence was longer. "Maybe that's the point. Maybe I don't want to crush Julie's spirit. But I don't know how else to reach her. I . . . I don't know how to get her to respect *me,* either."

Although there were many ideas here, I suggested Dan zero in on the word that seemed the most charged and important to him—a technique you can use yourself as you explore your own daydreams.

"You mean 'respect'?" he asked. I nodded. "For the next

few days, try to focus on the idea of 'respect,' " I told him. "What other daydreams do you come up with when you think about the word, for example?"

I reminded him that we weren't talking about actions he should or would take in the real world. All of the movement needed to be in his imagination, where he would go as far as he could to invent new scenarios around respect. It took some time, but the results were powerful.

In a later meeting, Dan told me, "Well, I imagined talking to my father and telling him forcefully that he *had* to listen to me, and then having him respond that he had always been *so* proud of me, that he would of course listen to me. And I put together scenarios with Julie, and even with Stacy, my wife, who doesn't always act so respectful, either. Oh, I had a grand old time. I saw myself presenting some new ideas to my boss and had him express awe at my understanding of the situation. . . ." He grinned.

"But you know what else was interesting? While I was doing all this, I started to think about Julie again. About how she used to be the one person in my life who *always* respected me. It was such a surprise when she started putting me down. She sounded *just* like my dad. . . . I didn't know how to react. . . ." He was silent for a minute, thinking. "I still don't. It still feels like a surprise . . . and a betrayal. . . ."

Dan had just put into words how hard it was for him—as it is for most of us—to cope with the changes and conflicts that develop between every parent and child at some point. Julie was growing up and, as a normal consequence of her development, was no longer idealizing her father. For Dan, however, her new-found disdain for both of her parents brought not only the painful loss of his place as his daughter's hero, but a reminder of old, hurtful questions about his self-worth. No wonder thoughts of Julie cropped up at work, where he frequently struggled with the question of respect. And, for the same reasons, he was now bombarding himself with memories of his lifelong struggle with his father over the same issue.

He asked himself a crucial question: "Do I know my daughter at all? Does she know me?" He was silent for a minute, then continued quietly, "I think the answer to both of those questions is no. So how do we get to know each other?" He paused. "I don't want to lose her."

I suggested that he try to discover some new daydreams. Could he, for example, imagine ways he might work on getting to know his daughter and helping her to know him? The daydreams he came up with in answer to this question were sometimes funny, sometimes painful, often completely unrealistic. But I encouraged him not to take them literally, to let himself play with different scenarios until something really felt right to him. Gradually, he began to notice that the daydreams that made the most sense were the simplest ones. He said, "I keep thinking about starting with the basics. Like just standing my ground. I don't deserve to be talked to the way she talks to me. I'm not a doormat. I do not want to slap her; but I *do* want her to talk to me like I'm a human being." And, again, "I want to talk to her like she's a human being, too. Not a little monster, and not a female version of my father. I want to find out who she really is."

These realizations didn't lead Dan to a sudden reconciliation with his daughter. In fact, his first attempts to relate differently to her ended in a series of resounding battles between them. "But my daydreams are different now," he said. "I *imagine* us fighting. I don't see these arguments as a sign of lack of respect. It's part of the whole painful picture." He grinned wryly. "I guess that's what you'd call a mature daydream?"

Like Dan, many of us unconsciously use our daydreams to close off parts of ourselves. By doing so, we also close down our options for coping with new situations, often choosing to treat them as though they are the same as ones we have already dealt with (not always particularly well). As Dan worked to explore familiar daydreams, he also began to do some mental gardening: to weed out old, unhelpful images and to nourish the seeds of other, less familiar daydreams. Some of these daydreams then became the foundation for Dan to explore expanded alternatives, new ways to cope with the changes that were accompanying his daughter's growth—and that are an inevitable part of everyone's life.

Among the many functions these new daydreams served was one Dan had never even realized he needed: they helped him move out of the narrow image of himself as a person who could not *expect* to be respected. Many of us get stuck in these kinds of rigid self-images. Just as Dan did, you can use your daydreams as clues to some of these fixed views of yourself. Once you have discovered some of your own static images, you can also use your daydreams to solve problems: to open up new ways of being with people, and as a result to discover new ways of being with yourself.

In the next story, you'll see how one woman closed off a whole group of feelings because they didn't fit with her need to define herself as a "good girl." As you read, keep your mind alert to the ways you, too, narrow your range of possibilities: what partial truths do you cling to, closing out the rest of the story, in order to protect or maintain a certain image of yourself?

THE "GOOD GIRL": STUCK IN PAINFUL DAYDREAMS

Even when your daydreams are symptoms of a serious psychological problem they can be crucial aids in your quest for self-knowledge and your goal of making significant changes in your life. This is how it worked for Margie, who suffered from a phobic disorder. Although she was on a medication that was helping, like many people she needed to do some personal work as well.

The operative word for Margie was "soft": from her dark-brown curls to her brown eyes and gentle voice, she was the epitome of muted delicacy. But not in her daydreams. They were filled with horror stories—images of her loved ones mutilated and dying in terrible car accidents or robbed and murdered, suddenly and painfully and graphically destroying their lives and hers at once. She seemed to collect frightening tales that confirmed her worst fears: a friend whose husband dropped dead of a heart attack on the tennis court, leaving his wife with three children under the age of thirteen; an acquaintance whose son died of leukemia; and another whose daughter was killed while biking home from school. Unable to put these fears out of her mind, she worried anytime her husband or sons were out of her sight. "When John, my husband, goes to the grocery store, I live in dread till he returns. When I hear an ambulance during the day, I imagine that it's for one of my children.

"I'm a *lawyer*," she said with frustration, "but I haven't worked in eight years. I *can't* work. Can you imagine me trying to argue a case?" She giggled nervously. "I saw a phobia specialist, but he wasn't able to help me. Maybe it was my fault. He told me I have always had difficulties separating from my family; that that was why the fears got worse when Timmy, my youngest, started school last year. That part made some sense, although I'm not sure I *always* have trouble separating. But I was turned off when he told me I was lucky, that some people are so paralyzed by fears like mine that they can't leave the house alone. I don't *feel* lucky. Just because I can go out doesn't mean I don't hurt all the time.

"I've had these fears all my life. When I was little, I worried about my parents' being killed in a car accident or having a heart attack or getting mugged. On nights that they went out, I would stay awake until I heard their car come into the driveway.

"It's so hard to explain. Maybe I'm a masochist—I just like to be in pain," she sighed.

I've never been convinced that such formulations explain anything, and I shared this thought with Margie. Instead, I recommended that we rummage through her daydreams to see what meanings we could discover; and of course I encouraged her to keep a daydream journal. I told her to pay special attention to where she was and what she was doing when the disturbing daydreams appeared.

"They come from out of nowhere," she replied. "I don't think anything in particular triggers them."

As we've noticed, this is often how it feels when we first begin to open up our world of daydreams, but gradually, as we follow the train of thought that accompanies any daydream images, we may discover that these fantasies have surprising sources and definite triggers. They don't, after all, come from nowhere. As Margie started to pay attention to the details of her daydreams, she was fascinated by what she found.

"The other day," she said in her soft voice, nervously twisting a strand of hair between two fingers, "I went out to the park to jog. I used to be on the track team in high school—I was pretty good, I guess, but more important to me was how much I enjoyed it." Her voice contained a note of wistfulness as she continued. "I don't run so much now. I'm not in shape, and I can't do more than a mile these days. And I jiggle in all the wrong places. It's nearly six years since my second child was born, but I just can't seem to take the weight off.

"But when I *can* get myself to go out for a run, I generally feel much better. Anyway, that day I managed to get out to the park to jog. I moved slowly, but at least I was moving. I was even feeling pretty good, despite the flab bouncing around on my thighs and butt, when I suddenly started to imagine some sort of accident happening at the school. I couldn't kick the thought, so I cut my run short and went home to check my answering machine in case something had happened and the school was trying to reach me.

"I know it's ridiculous, but each time these attacks come over me, I'm convinced that I'm having a premonition, and I have to get home to be available for the phone call that I'm sure will come. I never recognize that it's one of my attacks until hours later. Sometimes I have a terribly strong urge to drive to the school to check on the kids, but I don't go, because I don't want to miss that phone call—not to mention that they would die of embarrassment if they saw me there checking up on them. So I stay there at home, waiting, sometimes for two or three hours, till the fear passes.

"Here's the interesting thing. *This* time, as I was waiting for the phone to ring, I tried to remember what had happened in the moments before I got the 'anxiety attack.' At first I couldn't think of anything, except that I'd been running. But then I remembered that a woman I know from the neighborhood passed me just a minute or two before the attack. She waved and I waved back, and then she ran on ahead of me." She paused, then wondered out loud, "Now, what in the world could that have had to do with my fears?"

I asked Margie if she could remember any of her thoughts as the neighbor passed her.

"Not really," she started, then interrupted herself. "Well, except that I was thinking that she was in much better shape than me. I remember saying to myself that she was younger and better-looking than me; and then I had this funny thought that no man would look at me if she was around. I was surprised that I had that thought—it seemed disloyal to John. I'm not even interested in any other men. But the main thing I thought about was how I'd let my body get so out of shape. I felt terrible about myself, ashamed and embarrassed that she could pass me so easily. And I guess it was right after that that I started to think that something had happened to one of the children."

Slowly, thoughtfully, looking at me as she continued to twist her hair around her fingers, she went on: "Maybe that fear was my way of punishing myself for wanting another man to look at me?" she said tentatively. "What do you think?"

I told her that that seemed to be a real possibility. "Most daydreams have several different meanings," I said. "We can only tell what they are, and which ones are most significant, by observing your subsequent thoughts and your feelings over time."

"Well, my thoughts have just gone in a completely different direction," she said when I finished. I encouraged her to put them into words, since important information often appears in such apparently disconnected ideas.

"I was just thinking about the lunch I had—or, rather, didn't have—with Karen, my 'big' sister, the other day. We haven't seen each other for a while, because she works long, crazy hours, and I was looking forward to catching up, *and* to seeing what she's done in her living room, which she's just finished redecorating. She's been talking about it for ages. She's got an incredible eye for color and style—and the money to back her up. I got there and saw her new furniture and rug, which were just magnificent. She talked for a while about why she chose what she did, and what different people had said about her choices, and then we went to the kitchen to get the dishes out for lunch. I think maybe I heard an ambulance in the background, I'm not sure. But I suddenly got scared that something had happened to one of the boys. Karen tried to talk me out of it, but it was useless. I tore back home to sit by the phone and wait for 'the call.' "

She paused, a puzzled look on her face. "You know, I just had this weird thought about my old job, basically wondering if it was still open. It's not so strange that I would start to think about work; I mean, since Timmy started school last fall, I've thought a lot about going back to work, but I have to get these fears under control first. In fact, that's one of the reasons I went to the phobia specialist: we need the money. . . . But I wouldn't go back to my old job if I was starving to death! So why would I think about it right now?"

Why indeed? I encouraged Margie to try to put into words whatever came into her mind in order to discover some of the hidden meanings of this new daydream. "I hated that job. When I left there, I decided never to go back to a large law firm. It almost turned me off law completely, not to mention the terrible things it did to my ego. I worked there for almost eight horrible years after I passed the bar. The hours were horrendous, but not nearly as bad as the way we were treated.

"Fran, my best friend, who went through law school with me, was the only reason I survived. She and I provided a lot of support for one another. We moved up the ranks together. Then, about a year before I got pregnant with Mark, my first child, she got promoted and I didn't. I was *really* happy for her. She absolutely deserved the promotion. But she moved to a new office, and I felt left behind. . . .

"How weird! I just remembered a dream I had last night, when I was asleep. Or really just a piece of a dream. It's such a little thing—should I tell you about it?" I nodded. "Well, all I remember is that I was little, maybe four or five years old, and I was getting ready to get on a school bus. That's it."

I asked Margie how she felt in the dream. "I think I was excited. Oh, I know, I had the thought, 'Now *I'm* a big kid!' " She was silent for a minute, her eyes almost closed as she turned her thoughts inward. When she looked back at me, she said, "My mind just sort of went in two directions at once. I don't know which way to go."

I suggested that she list both sets of thoughts first, without going into a great deal of detail, and then we could come back and fill in some of the finer points. This is a useful technique anytime you have a number of thoughts and associations to a situation or a daydream. You can write your thoughts down, in a list, then come back and explore the ideas at your leisure. This apparently simple step will keep you from forgetting one train of associations as you pursue another—and eventually might lead to some important connections you could otherwise miss.

"Okay," Margie replied, taking a deep breath. "One set of thoughts went with something my mom has told me about. I don't remember it at all, but she says that when we were kids, before I started school, I used to have a major temper tantrum every morning when Karen got on the school bus and left me behind!" She smiled. "I guess we can see the connection to my dream about the bus. Especially when I tell you the other set of thoughts. They were about putting Timmy, my little one, on the school bus for the first time."

Now that she had outlined the two paths her thoughts had taken, I encouraged Margie to try to talk about her next ideas randomly, as they came to her mind. Again, this is something you can do as well: once you've made your list, let your thoughts go where they will. They may take you somewhere interesting on their own. If not, look for themes in your next images and ideas, and then ask yourself what thoughts you have about these themes.

Margie's next thoughts seemed not to tell us anything new. But gradually, as we searched for a motif that ran through these and some of her other ideas, we made some important discoveries that helped explain her worries in a new way.

"All my life I felt like there was something wrong with me because I was behind Karen. Even though I knew intellectually that it was just because I'd been born later, I interpreted it as being some sort of sign of my inferiority. I worked super-hard in school to 'catch up' with her. I was actually a much better student than Karen was, but somehow that didn't seem to count: I still felt like she was better at everything than I was. I never have felt like I really was a big kid!"

Margie hesitated, nervously twisting her wedding ring on her finger. She glanced up at me and asked, "Is this going anywhere? It doesn't seem to be getting us any closer to getting rid of those daydreams."

I reassured her that, even though we couldn't see where we were going to end up, we were learning some important details both about how she functioned and how she organized her experience. "You may not 'get rid' of your disturbing daydreams," I told her, "at least not right away. But what we learn will help you understand and cope with them. And that understanding should also, eventually, diminish the power the daydreams have over you."

I told her that it seemed to me that she had just interrupted a rather meaningful flow of associations with her question about whether or not we were getting anywhere. "I wonder if that interruption is your way of slowing down the process, maybe because we're getting closer to some feelings that you're not terribly comfortable with?"

"Oh, I don't know, I'm just not so sure this is working for me," Margie replied with a sigh.

I told her that the exact opposite might actually be true: perhaps she was beginning to put something together at the edges of her conscious thought, and she was unconsciously afraid of what she was going to see. Without realizing it, Margie was slowing things down, so that the emerging information didn't suddenly overwhelm her (so that she couldn't use it at all) or cause her to put up even stronger walls against the "unthought known" that she was beginning to think about. This "pulling on the reins" is a normal part of the process of understanding the meanings of your daydreams, and it needs to be respected.

In our next meeting, Margie told me that she had thought a

lot about what we had been discussing. "The other set of thoughts I had was about Timmy—how he's growing up so fast. I feel like I'm unnecessary now. Actually, that phobia specialist I saw said that was the problem: I was having difficulties separating from him. He thought I'd probably had troubles separating from my parents, too. It does make sense. He's got his good buddies in first grade, and he's very attached to his father, and his big brother. . . . While I was thinking about those things, something else came into my mind. It's that I worry about Timmy's relationship with Mark. I'm afraid that he feels inadequate—like I did with Karen. I started thinking about how *competitive* they are. Why can't they just accept each other and themselves?"

I asked Margie to tell me the first things that came into her mind when she thought of being competitive. She was silent for a moment. "I don't know. . . . I'm not a competitive person. That was always one of my problems at my job. Unless," she said slowly, "unless you think feeling like I couldn't catch up with Karen was being competitive . . ."

It was, of course. Margie was beginning to see that her sons were able to compete openly, whereas she had stifled her own competitive strivings by viewing herself as inferior and inadequate.

"I just started to think about how I felt when Fran got promoted at work. Don't get me wrong—I was very happy for her—but I felt like it meant something was wrong with me, since we'd both started at the same time. . . . You know, that's actually why I stopped running competitively. When I lost a race, it was like I lost *everything good* about myself. And I hated the person who beat me, like they had *taken* something away from me. It was a terrible feeling. I didn't like myself when I felt that way. It made me feel ugly."

"Ugly" is often a code word women use for feeling unfeminine. When you discover emotions you have pushed out of your consciousness, you might want to ask yourself if you have discon-

nected from them because they aren't acceptable in your definition of femininity or masculinity. As we've seen, these subtle limi-
tations are often part of daydream imagery. Though it will usually
not be the only reason you have not allowed those feelings into
your conscious thinking, you might find, as did Larry, Mona, and
Margie, that your feminine or masculine identity is a significant
factor, and one worth bringing into the light of day.

As Margie kept track of her various thoughts, she began to
see that she often "stuffed down" thoughts that, as she put it,
seemed "ugly, aggressive, and unfeminine—the opposite of the
'good girl' I was always trying to be. This is awful. But now that
I'm thinking about it, I realize that I actually did have a really
aggressive thought at Karen's right before I had the anxiety attack.
It was something about bringing my sons over and seeing what
happens to her beautiful new furniture. Two active boys . . . it
would be pretty bad. That wasn't the only thing I thought, you
know—it was beautiful, and I was very pleased for her—but I
guess I just wish I could have something like it, or . . . at least
something that I felt good about."

She stopped in surprise. "Did you hear what I just said? I had
the anxiety attack after I imagined bringing the boys over to
destroy Karen's beautiful new furniture. I guess it *was* a way of
punishing myself for having such a horrible thought." Later, when
she was out running again, Margie remembered that when her
neighbor had passed her the other day she had had a momentary
urge to stick her foot out and trip her. "Maybe I get these attacks
so that I don't *do* something horrible," she told me. "I never
thought of myself as such a competitive, envious person before.
Ugh. It's not a pretty picture."

Although Margie didn't like what she saw, she was in the
process of making a significant breakthrough with this new
knowledge about herself. As with Mona, Margie's sense of herself
as a victim kept her from having to face some of her other, less

acceptable feelings. Unfortunately, in order to maintain a view of herself as sweetly innocent, she had to avoid her *healthy* competitive strivings; she could not integrate either these or her hostile, envious feelings into her overall identity.

As Margie got in touch with some of these previously unacceptable emotions, she began to see that she had always felt it was "bad" to compete, that her anxiety attacks often nipped in the bud any potential competitive strivings on her part—and that they also kept at bay the thought that anyone else might be competitive with her.

With some difficulty, she told me, "I see now that, as much as I dislike feeling envious of someone else, I hate even more the idea that someone else might be envious of *me*." And it was still more complicated. "Karen has always wanted children. It's been terribly painful for her not to have them. And I got pregnant easily, exactly when I wanted to, in my thirties, after my career and my marriage were solid and I'd had time to play around first, too. I've never put it this way to myself before, but I think I felt guilty . . . and kept waiting to be punished . . . I guess by having something terrible happen to one of the boys, or to John. . . ."

Margie's daydreams about potential tragedy did not magically disappear; but as she pursued her thoughts about them, she became more adept at acknowledging the complex feelings and thoughts that frequently triggered them. As a result, these painful daydreams gradually lost some of their punch, and tentatively, with great anxiety, Margie began to dip her toe into some activities that had previously seemed closed off to her. She began to exercise more regularly, and even to laugh at herself when she got angry at someone who was in better shape. She joined a book club, and spent more time with her sister (Margie now understood that she had unconsciously been working hard at *not* getting together with Karen). With each step, she gained the self-confidence that would eventually make it possible for her to fulfill another daydream—going back to work.

———————

Even though your daydreams may not have the same para-
lyzing effect as Margie's, they may still keep you from seeing and
acknowledging some of your potential, opportunities you don't
even realize are there. They may contribute to your unconscious
repetition of long-term patterns of interaction, patterns based on
old, unexamined beliefs about yourself and the first people you
related to—your parents, siblings, and other relatives.

In the next story, you will see how daydreams can either
narrow or expand your vision in a different way. Like Margie,
Annie only saw part of the story in her memories and daydreams
of her family. For her, this partial truth provided much-needed
protection from hurtful information; but at the same time, it made
it nearly impossible for her to deal with a painful family crisis.

ONE-DIMENSIONAL IMAGES: FAMILY DAYDREAMS
THAT LIMIT TODAY'S RELATIONSHIPS

"My dad's got Alzheimer's," Annie said in her surprisingly deep
voice. "It's hard to tell you what it's like. He was such a wonderful man. I can't stand to see what he's become." Tears began to
stream down her face. A tiny woman with a thick mane of elegantly coiffed white hair, she became almost fierce as she spoke of
her father's past. "He was always such a happy man—so cheerful,
so full of life, so filled with wonderful plans. He always had a
scheme up his sleeve: a way he was finally going to make enough
money to retire for good." She stopped to blow her nose. "Talk
about daydreams," she said through her tears. "Dad was full of
them. To give you just one example: for as long as I can
remember, he's been building a sailboat in our backyard, a boat he
was going to sail around the world when he retired.

"Now he can't remember anything. He doesn't know any of
us, not me or my mother or my younger brother; not even his

grandchildren, who he *adored*. Most of the time he doesn't even remember his own name." She sobbed into her hands. "I can't stand watching him like this.

"I visit him in the nursing home every day, even though he doesn't always know me and doesn't remember that I was there. But it must make it better for him, don't you think?" She didn't wait for an answer. "It breaks my heart. As soon as I get there, he tells me he wants to go home. Then he crosses over to the window and says something about the direction the wind's blowing. You can't have a conversation with him, but I think he's thinking about sailing." Her delicate features lit up with a smile. "I used to sail with him all the time. Mother refused to get in a boat with him, she said she got seasick. I think she just didn't want to be with him. I *loved* being out there with him. He knew so much. He could talk about all of the sea life, and point out different fish, turtles, birds, sea grasses. . . . He was so patient, such a good teacher. It was from him that I got my love of knowledge . . . and of the sea.

"I can't believe my mother put him in that place. She said she couldn't take care of him. It's not that she *couldn't*, but that she *won't*; she's got her own life to live, and she's not going to let anything or anyone interfere with it. She's always been this way, not just with Daddy but with my brother and me, too.

"I remember once telling her I'd gotten a part in a school play. I was *so* excited, so pleased with myself. 'Ah yes,' she said, 'I played that part when I was much younger than you.' That was her whole reaction. She didn't get excited for me, didn't offer to help me, just needed to let me know *she'd* already done it—and better than I could, anyway.

"My brother, Robbie, and I have tried to figure out how we could take Daddy in to live with one of us. But Robbie's divorced, living with three kids in a tiny apartment; and I don't have room in my apartment for a cat, let alone another person."

Again she started to sob, covering her face with her hands. "I feel like my life is over," she whispered. "And I *hate* my mother.

"It's so horrible to see him there, so confused, so alone. I can't stand to see him like this, it's so terrible. Sometimes I don't want to go to that . . . that *place* at all, but I force myself. He needs to have company, even if he doesn't recognize us. Not Mother, though. She's going on a trip, says she needs to take care of herself. Boy, that's unusual! I don't mean to be sarcastic, but it makes me really angry. Poor Daddy."

Brushing her thick silver hair off her face, she went on. "Sometimes I wish that *Mother* was the one with Alzheimer's. I know that's terrible, but it's what I think about. I think about killing myself and Daddy. Nobody would miss me, and it would put him out of his misery. He seems so very sad at that home. I can see it in his eyes. I wish I could take him home with me. But he should be with my mother, not with me!"

Both rage and sorrow saturated Annie's every word as she described her daydreams. Her feelings were not hidden—that wasn't the problem—but she was having trouble coping with the loss of the father she had adored and admired. Understanding the meanings of her daydreams would not take away Annie's pain, but it could make the pain easier to manage. In fact, Annie told me later that just talking about her feelings to a neutral person, someone not in her family, made them more tolerable. This is an important lesson to remember: if your feelings are so painful or unpleasant that they feel unbearable, even if they're completely straightforward and available, it can help to talk them out with a friend or write them down in your daydream journal. Feelings have a way of changing, sometimes subtly and sometimes drastically, simply as a result of being expressed in words.

But daydreams can also help you manage these feelings. Annie's daydreams, like her feelings, were direct and to the point. She disliked the intensity of her rage and her sorrow; she wanted to "do" something about these feelings, but she certainly was neither disguising nor squelching them.

I asked Annie to search her mind for pleasant memories of both of her parents.

At first, she could only think of negative images of her mother and positive ones of her father. But in an attempt to follow the "assignment," she pulled out old photograph albums. "And they brought back some of the good times—not just with my parents, but with my brother, too, and with my grandparents, and my aunts and uncles, and cousins. . . . You know, they also brought back some of the bad times with my father. He wasn't always so loving. As I looked at the pictures, I remembered how withdrawn he could be, especially when his schemes didn't work out—something that happened fairly often, as a matter of fact. I even remembered times when I cried to my mother that he didn't love me at all. And I remember how she held me and stroked my hair and told me that he loved me, he just wasn't always able to show it."

The next time Annie saw her mother, she was surprised to find that she felt less antagonistic. "I found myself remembering how she had comforted me when I was younger; but not only that, I realized that things must not have always been easy for her. Who comforted her when Daddy withdrew from her, when they ran out of money because he'd put it all into some project that flopped? You know," she said with wonder in her deep voice, "I'd forgotten that Mother had to go to work as a maid, because we had no money and she had no job skills."

Annie's relationship with her mother didn't change dramatically as a result of these memories. But this brief contact with her tender feelings for her mother had a subtle yet surprising impact. "I don't really understand it, but I'm not in such a rage that I can't talk to her at all anymore. I can even see her point of view a little more clearly, and that makes me less angry. Yesterday, for example, we were both at the nursing home, and Daddy kept saying he wanted to go home. And Mother said, 'He said that even when he was home. At my Alzheimer's group, they tell me that it's a normal complaint. They just don't feel like they're at home wherever they are.'

"My first reaction was to think, 'Oh yeah, you're rationalizing away your guilt once again.' But then I flashed on that image of Mother comforting me, and I remembered that it wasn't all black and white. It's not Mother's fault that Daddy has Alzheimer's. She must be feeling a lot of her own pain. I even felt glad that she had her group to help her through this time."

Annie began to see that her idealistic daydreams about her father kept her from dealing with some information she didn't want to remember. Similarly, her daydreams about her mother only told part of the story. She explained to me, "I had everything in absolutes: she was all bad, he was all good. But that isn't the way it really was. I can't say that my mother and I have suddenly gotten close, but I certainly do have a different picture of the situation. It's hard for her. I see that now. . . . But it's still hard for Daddy, and I still feel terrible about that. I guess I was holding on to the good memories about him to keep from losing him completely. And . . . and maybe my angry feelings at Mother helped me deal with my own guilt about not doing something to rescue him. . . .

"But . . . it seems to me that . . . it might be helpful to talk to her more about what we're both going through. Maybe we could be a little closer. Maybe I don't have to lose both of my parents right now. I'm not so angry at her; I guess I'm angry that life is like this, but it doesn't feel so overwhelming right now."

Annie's rage wasn't hidden, but, because it wasn't something she was able to talk about, all of her other feelings and thoughts were practically obliterated by it. Once able to talk about these terrible feelings and daydreams, she was also able to reconnect to other aspects of her experience—other memories, daydreams, feelings, and thoughts. Her sense of herself and her world became more complex, and more real.

Splitting off certain feelings from others—dwelling on emotional reactions that make sense to you, feelings with which you're familiar, while attempting to push away vague and more disturbing feelings that don't make as much sense—is an attempt to cope with the complexity of *having* so many contradictory or at least ambiguous emotions at once. It is an impulse to simplify, to manage the force of the whole spectrum of your feelings by blocking some of them out. But oversimplifying any experience makes it less meaningful, less resolvable, because you have to close off part of yourself. You may end up feeling a vague, chronic anxiety that seems to have no source. You are also limiting the rainbow of your emotions to one or two colors—obviously blocking out most of the rainbow. This puts a lid on the full, rich range of what's really happening inside you.

Annie still felt awful about her father's illness and her mother's way of handling it. But she began to be able to cope with these feelings differently. Now she felt not only rage but sadness and loss; at the same time, however, she was able to remember more of her own life, more of the complexity that made it possible for her to tolerate what was happening to her now.

What images of your family—and yourself in relation to that family—do you carry around with you? How have (or haven't) your images of your family changed over time?

The following exercise will give you a chance to see just how much your images *do* change over time; and it will help you open up some of those old daydreams about your family, so you can let go of unchanging images that keep you in old ruts. As you work on these exercises, look especially for daydreams that close down or cut off some of the complexity of your experience. And then see if you can color in the images— move them from black and white to multicolored, from one-dimensional to multidimensional.

EXERCISE:

PUTTING THE COLORS BACK IN THE RAINBOW—COLORING IN YOUR FAMILY PICTURES

1. Think of a family member—it doesn't matter who, although it's best to choose the first one you think of. (It's fine even if it's Great-Aunt Grace, whom you saw only once in your life, as long as she's the first person to come to your mind.)

2. Now turn to another blank page in your daydream diary and write down the first four or five words that come to your mind when you think of that family member.

Perhaps you think of Aunt Grace's old-lady smell. Write that down. Next you think of stale doughnuts (because, the one time you visited her, that's what she served). Write that down, too. Then, you don't know why, you think of dried flowers and vodka. You know Aunt Grace couldn't have served you vodka— you were only seven years old—and you can't imagine that she and your mother ate stale doughnuts and drank liquor, but there it is. That's the next word that comes to your mind. And you haven't got the slightest idea why you thought of dried flowers.

3. What else do you recall about that episode in your life—the summer you were seven, let's say, when your family traveled to Kansas to visit relatives you had never met? Do you remember fighting with your brother and sister in the back seat of the car for the whole long drive? What do you recall of your parents at that time? Your brother? Sister? Other relatives?

4. If you have the opportunity, check with other members of your family to find out what they remember. How similar are your recollections? How are they different?

Also, if you can, look at old family photographs from that time. Do they remind you of anything you'd forgotten? Do they confirm your memories? Or are the pictures they offer different from the ones in your mind?

5. Go back to the list of words you made when you first thought of the relative. Do you have any better sense of what they mean? Let your mind wander a little. Your thoughts may take you to an explanation of the odd associations you first had.

For example, perhaps Aunt Grace smoked cigarettes. You had forgotten that; but the dried flowers remind you of tobacco, and you associate cigarettes with having a drink (of liquor). And then you remember that on this trip to your mother's family your father went out for a "walk" one night and didn't get back until quite late; now you're pretty sure he went to a local bar to get away from the family. You even heard him and your mother arguing about it when he got back. She told him he smelled like smoke—another connection, perhaps, to Aunt Grace and her "old-lady smell" in your earlier associations. But at the time you didn't put it together. You were having a great summer. It didn't occur to you that there was any tension in the house.

Don't be too surprised if you start to find contradictions and puzzles in your new memories. We're not looking for all the so-called problems you've hidden away, and I'm not even suggesting that your new memories will be more valid than your old ones. We are, however, looking to add complexity and richness to your images of your family members. For example, it didn't occur to you at the time that your father might be uncomfortable with your mother's family, but now it makes perfect sense. Aunt Grace was, you have learned as you talk to your mother and father about this episode, furious with him for taking your mother so far away from her. He had come for this visit because he felt it was important for you kids—and your mother—to see her family, but they were driving him crazy.

Although these elaborations of old, almost forgotten memories may not have tremendous obvious significance at the moment, they will increase the dimensions of your understanding—of your family, yourself, and even other people in your life. And as you expand your capacity to see the complexity of any experience, you will automatically extend your capacity to function in the external world.

Annie, for example, remembered the summer she was ten as idyllic. She recalled those wonderful occasions when she and her father had gone sailing. But when she looked at the old photos from that time, she was surprised to see how withdrawn her father looked, always standing a little apart from the family group, and frequently with a sour look on his face. She spoke to her brother about it, and he reminded her that their father had lost everything in a business venture that summer.

"It doesn't eliminate my memories of the special times with him," Annie said, "but it does add something to the picture. Something I'd cut out completely."

Annie was beginning to see aspects of both of her parents that she had pushed out of her conscious memory. The words "withdrawn" and "moody" were not in her original description of her father, but they went on the list after the pictures jogged some more colors into her memories. And, similarly, she added words like "hardworking" and "lonely" to her list of words about her mother. Though the image she now had of each of her parents wasn't as simple as the one she had carried around with her for years, it was richer—and made her life richer as a result.

"I've always been so angry," she said to me. "I get into fights with everyone—my doctor's receptionist, my next-door neighbor, my local butcher. Since I've been doing this work on my family images, I seem to be a little less irritable. Sometimes I can actually see more than one side to the picture—I can even feel some sympathy for the other person. And that makes me feel less angry."

FAMILY CONFLICT

In our daydreams of the "perfect" family, most of us imagine a family *without conflict*. In fact, conflict is a natural part of every family relationship. Conflict allows each of us to define his or her own space, and identity, and this makes it possible for us to recognize differences and similarities. When recognized and respected, family conflict becomes the touchstone for our negotiations with all the people we meet in the course of the rest of our lives. Just as each of us struggles with conflicting goals internally, we must all make some sort of peace with the *lack of peace* in our family constellations: with our children, our spouses, our parents, our siblings. Every relationship is made up of a complex interweaving of the tangled web of feelings—hopes and wishes, fears and anxieties—that constitute the internal world of each member of the relationship. So how in the world can a family, even a family of two, be conflict-free?

The daydream of a "perfect" family—loving, stressless, conflict-free, whatever—is like the daydream of a perfect romance or a perfect self: a fantasy that protects but also harms.

In this chapter we have also seen that internal conflict—like

Margie's struggle against her "bad" (competitive) feelings—can reflect conflict between people as well; and external conflict, like Dan's struggle with his daughter, can equally well represent internal, personal battles. Your daydreams are your tools for exploring these struggles, and eventually for finding ways to manage the conflicts, to make compromises, to stand your ground—in other words, to choose from a variety rather than a limited set of responses. And as you will see in the next chapter, they provide an invaluable arena for exploring and working through some of the most painful conflicts of our lives.

CHAPTER NINE

When Bad Things Happen: Using Daydreams to Cope

MUCH AS WE may want to believe in fairy-tale endings, life is, in general, a mixture of good and bad—some sweetness and some pain, some happiness and some sadness, some raging turmoil and some peace—in different amounts at different times.

Perhaps you feel that your pain is far more overwhelming, and lasts longer, than your happy or even your pleasant times. Or do you feel that your burdens are heavier than those of other people you know? On the other hand, you might have as much trouble with good feelings as some people do with bad. Strange as it may seem, perhaps you are more comfortable, and even feel safer, when things aren't good (at least then, you may say to yourself, whether consciously or unconsciously, they can't get worse!).

Each of these moods is connected to your daydream world, tied to an intricately woven pattern of stories and assumptions that help you cope with the complex and sometimes difficult process of living. As usual, these attempts to adapt to the pains and pressures of your life can either end up interfering with your ability to cope, or enhance that ability.

In this chapter, we will look at how daydreams that have kept you stuck in the pain can be turned—just slightly—so that you can get on with your life. As you know, sometimes it takes just a slight shift in perspective to make a difference; a tiny crack in a window can dramatically change the landscape you see out that window.

How does this work?

For one thing, pain is often intensified by unarticulated and unexplored assumptions you make about the causes of your pain. As you explore your daydreams, you will bring some of your assumptions out into the light of day—and that in itself can lead to significant shifts in perspective. But there are other factors that can make the normal suffering that is part of everyone's life even more difficult. As you read the following stories, you will see that—like everything else—painful feelings are responses not only to life events, but also to the complex, interrelated, and often conflicting stories we tell ourselves to explain or cope with our experiences. Your daydreams, again, are gateways to those stories.

Of course, we'd all rather not go through such difficult times; but if we don't let ourselves feel such emotions, at least to some extent, we end up suffering more. This doesn't mean wallowing in self-pity, depression, resentment, or grief. And sometimes closing down the system—stopping all feeling—is a necessary and adaptive response to overwhelming suffering. But putting your daydreams into words and looking at some of the thoughts that follow them can actually, ultimately, lessen the pain enough so that you can get through it. In the stories in this chapter, you will see how daydreams can help you avoid your pain—and you will learn ways to turn this process around, to use your daydreams to understand the hurt, to get through the hard times, move on, and live.

Once again, the particular pain or emotional difficulty you face may not be perfectly reflected in this chapter. But as you read the stories and do the exercises, asking yourself the questions I ask the people in these examples, try to tease out the threads that apply to the specifics of your own life. And keep a lookout for new daydreams—fantasies that will emerge quietly, slowly—that will provide your life with new richness, and perhaps even with new direction.

WHAT HAPPENED TO THE FOUNTAIN OF YOUTH?
COPING WITH MIDDLE AGE

No matter how "mature" we may be, most of us tend to forget that being beautiful and rich is no protection against hurt—including the pain of loss and of damaged self-esteem. I was guilty of just such a failure when I first met Nora. A successful interior designer, she was forty-nine years old, breathtakingly beautiful, elegantly dressed . . . and as I quickly learned, completely miserable.

"My doctor sent me to you," she said in a voice without

emotion. "She says I'm depressed. I don't feel depressed. I just have all these physical symptoms. . . ." Her voice trailed off.

I encouraged her to go on. "I have stomach problems, but every test—and I've had them all—comes up negative. The doctors say there's nothing wrong, but I'm afraid I have some sort of stomach cancer that they just haven't been able to detect yet. I'm worried that, by the time they figure it out, it'll be incurable. And I have heart palpitations—I keep thinking I'm going to have a heart attack." She looked at me a little defensively. "It's not like I'm completely crazy—I do have a heart defect, something called a mitral-valve prolapse, that's causing the palpitations. But, again, the doctors—I've been to three different ones—say not to worry, it's not a sign of any serious problems. But how can I not worry? *Something's* not right with me. . . ."

For the next quarter of an hour, I listened as Nora droned on about numerous other physical complaints and concerns. Like the mitral-valve prolapse, each pain and worry had a physiological basis but, according to the doctors she had consulted, nothing that justified Nora's fears that she was dying.

However, as I told her, the physical difficulties were not simply "in her mind." They were in and about her body—bodily sensations which should not be disregarded. It was of course possible that they were symptoms whose underlying cause had yet to be discovered. But since she had been thoroughly examined by several different doctors, I suggested it could be useful to examine the messages that were contained in her concerns about her body: what unrecognized information about herself might be resting in her daydreams about her physical well-being?

Nora looked confused, so I searched around for an example. My eyes fell on her exquisite clothes: a long black tunic sweater of a rich, soft-looking fabric draped beautifully over an equally well-made long black skirt, and black boots of soft, supple leather. Though the outfit was lovely, it was striking in its starkness, the black unbroken even by a single piece of jewelry. She wore no makeup, and her sandy-colored hair was pulled back into a loose pony tail. On the chair next to her Nora had placed her black winter coat and a black handbag.

I asked if she could tell me the thoughts she'd had when she dressed that morning. "What made you choose this outfit? What were you thinking and feeling about yourself?"

She looked down at herself, as if to check what she was wearing. I had the sense that she almost had to look to know that her body was there.

"Oh," she said a little uncertainly, "I don't pay a lot of attention to what I put on these days. My boss said that I look like I'm going to a funeral. I guess that's what I feel like most of the time. I don't have very much energy—I think it's because of all of these physical problems—but the doctors don't agree. . . ." Again her voice drifted off.

I told her that these were daydream thoughts. For example, her boss's idea that she looked as if she were going to a funeral was perhaps indicative of some daydream of his, but it also evoked her own daydream connections: like the one that went with her *feeling* as though she were going to a funeral.

This observation seemed to spark a little life in her face for the first time since I had met her. "You know, that's weird—recently I've been thinking about my own funeral."

I asked her to tell me about those thoughts.

"Well . . . it's kind of embarrassing . . . but if you think it will help, I'll tell you. . . ." She carefully examined her hands, turning them over several times before she started to talk. "I have an image of my casket, covered with flowers, under a canopy in the cemetery. . . . And I imagine a small cluster of people there to say goodbye . . . my father and my son and daughter sobbing. . . ." I asked her if the image reminded her of anything else. "Do you know, it's exactly what it really looked like at my mother's funeral. Only my father looks like an old man in my daydreams—like he is now, not when Mother died, twenty-five years ago."

I encouraged Nora to put into words any thoughts that came into her mind now. "Well, I just thought that I'm planning to be cremated, so I won't *have* a casket. Do you think that this means something?"

I nodded and encouraged her to keep following her thoughts. She spoke slowly, but her voice wasn't as listless as it had been in the beginning. "Well . . . I'm thinking about this being the twenty-fifth anniversary of my mother's death. Could that be why I have the image of her funeral? It's hard to believe it's been that long. I still miss her." Nora's eyes filled with tears. "It's always been especially hard at particular times—like when I got married, and . . . and when I got divorced, too—I wanted her so much. And now, when everything seems to be going wrong, I wish she was here. My dad's a super person, but he's not Mom—he just couldn't give me what she did. And . . . it's even worse now that Dad's starting to show his age. I'm an only child, and my kids are grown—they have their own lives, they can't give me much support. . . ."

I saw Nora's face shut down again. In an expressionless voice she resumed talking about her physical symptoms. The pain and sadness had become too hard to bear, triggering a return to obsessive thoughts about her own physical well-being.

But even these thoughts had meaning, as we learned over time. Nora agreed, although at first doubtfully, to keep a daydream diary to log in the thoughts and feelings that her various physical complaints engendered in her. She was intrigued by the connections she began to discover.

For example, she told me, "I was feeling this pain in my stomach the other day. So I wrote down all my thoughts about that pain—and I came smack up against something I already knew but never thought had any psychological connection to my physical worries. Here's what it was: This isn't just the anniversary of Mother's death, but I'm the exact same age as she was when she first got sick. And what did she die of? Pancreatic cancer, which was diagnosed when she went to the doctor with terrible stomach pains . . . It *is* a real possibility that I could die of the same thing," she said slowly. "A lot of these illnesses are inherited."

Although following her daydreams had not, so far, lessened Nora's anxiety, it had given her more of a handle on some of the emotional baggage she was carrying with her.

She made another discovery as well. "My symptoms themselves aren't always so terrible," she told me. "I mean, the palpitations aren't pleasant, but when I can tell myself that they don't mean that I'm dying, that they're just part of this mitral-valve thing, and that they'll stop in a little while, they aren't unbearable. And the same thing with my stomach pains. They're not really bad. It's just that I'm so *worried* about myself that I'm constantly focusing on every physical detail. Every itch and twitch frightens me, because it may indicate some hidden cancer. . . ."

Nora had come face to face with another set of the daydreams and assumptions associated with her physical worries. Though this recognition did not completely alleviate her fears, it did shift her perspective enough so that she no longer panicked every time she felt a symptom.

Gradually, as she continued to keep her diary, to notice when and where she was when she had a daydream and her first thoughts after she wrote about it, Nora discovered other connections between feelings and thoughts that she had always seen as completely separate.

"My kids are growing so far away from me. After my divorce—nearly fifteen years ago—we had stormy times, but we always got through them. I guess this is just the way it's supposed to be . . . but I feel so lonely without them. And now . . . my husband has remarried, and he and his wife have just had a baby. And

Amanda, my daughter, and Joey, my son, seem to spend all of their time over at his house, playing with the baby. . . .

"I know it's a lot more fun to be there than to be with me. I'm just a mass of worries; and their father's happy, excited, fun to be around. And of course a baby is always wonderful. . . ."

She paused briefly, looking down as she smoothed out her long skirt. Then she went on. "Now, here's a daydream. I wish *I* could have another baby. Well, not really. I know how much work it is, and I feel too tired—too old. . . . But that's just it, isn't it? Life is so unfair. Joe Sr., my ex-husband, is a year and a half older than I am; but *he* can have another child. I can't. Since I started menopause, I feel like everything in me is dead . . . or dying. . . ."

I looked at her in astonishment. "You're going through menopause?" I asked. This was one set of symptoms she had not mentioned, and Nora looked closer to forty than fifty. I had completely forgotten her actual age.

"I know," she replied bitterly. "I don't look my age; but that doesn't change what's happening to my body. And I *hate* it—the hot flashes, the weight gain, the knowledge that I can't ever have another child. . . ." She gazed out the window. "But it's a fact of life. I'm closer to my own death than I am to my birth. It's a terrible place to be. . . ."

I acknowledged how painful these feelings were. She nodded, then looked back at me. "But what makes them even harder," she said, "is that so many painful things are going on at the same time. I'm aging, my children have grown away. . . . My father's aging, too. Soon I'm going to have to make some sort of arrangements for him to be taken care of . . . and I don't know how much longer he's got. . . ." She began to cry quietly. "One more painful daydream."

Most of us share some version of Nora's sadness and sense of loss as we move into middle age. For many of us, this is a time of reckoning. We have to come to grips with—sometimes for the first time—the knowledge that we will not be able to make all of our dreams come true. At the same time, we have to cope with tremendous multiple losses in a variety of personal relationships, our own physical condition, and, frequently, changes in our careers as well.

Exploring her daydreams could not change these realities for Nora, but she said that she was feeling more "grounded" since she had begun working with them. I asked if she could give me an example.

"Oh sure," she replied. "It's even connected to my physical symptoms. You see, since I've been paying attention to my day-dreams, I've noticed that I often start to feel physical symptoms and worry about my physical health right after I've seen my dad, or after I've talked with one of my children. It's been very helpful to think of these physical symptoms as my way of capturing my fears that I'm going to die, like we've discussed. But I'm finding out there's even more to them. The other day, after I left Dad, I didn't feel sad—I didn't feel anything. In fact, I literally couldn't feel my body for a few minutes. I got panicky, really scared. I thought it was a new symptom at first. And then I got heart palpitations. . . .

"Later, when I was writing in my daydream notebook, I realized that, as soon as the heart palpitations started, I could feel my body again! As uncomfortable as they were, those irregular, speedy heartbeats *grounded* me. It was almost like I was saying to myself, 'See? Your heart is beating. You're here.' " She turned to me, a puzzled look on her face. "Am I crazy?"

"Not by a long shot," I told her. In fact, she had just discovered another important meaning of the daydreams connected to her physical symptoms. As she pursued these thoughts, Nora realized that she had felt this "loss" of her body before.

"It's happened at work a few times. I'm feeling disconnected there, which is another loss for me. Work was always a place where I felt energized and good about myself. I know I'm good at

what I do. Or, rather, I always have known it till now. But now
. . . it seems like I've gotten too old there, too. The design firm I
work for just merged with another company, and although they
haven't said anything yet, it's pretty clear that I'm going to be
phased out. The other company has someone in the same position—a younger woman who doesn't cost as much as I do—and
they don't need both of us. Who would you keep if you were
trying to cut costs?

"Well, I've put out the word that I'm looking. And what
keeps coming back is that I'm too old. Not always that baldly, of
course, but that's the underlying message." Her voice trailed off as
she looked down at her hands, now resting quietly in her lap.

"No wonder you're feeling so low," I reflected back to her.
"Everything seems to be going wrong at once."

Nora nodded. "It's true. My daydreams are all about endings—my relationship with my kids, my dad, my career, my life as
a woman, my own death."

Shortly after this, Nora noticed a new daydream, one about
learning to play the piano. She said, "It's something I've always
wanted to do, but I've never had time. Why would I be thinking
about that now?"

Why indeed? Because, as Nora acknowledged the real suffering in her life, she began to lift her head out of the sludge—just
a little, but enough to have some daydream thoughts about life
beyond middle age. Gradually, over time, as Nora played with the
image of taking piano lessons, other ideas began to emerge. One
thought was that she had often said she would learn the piano
when she retired. "But I'm not *that* old," she protested. Then she
noticed something else. "Maybe it's a wish," she said. "Maybe all
these physical symptoms are my body's way of sending me
another message. I've been thinking for a while that I should slow
down; only I've been afraid of what that meant. But now, I'm
starting to have some other ideas. I can't afford not to work; but I
don't have a lot of expenses anymore, either. My house is paid for,

the kids are out of college. . . . I've always dreamed of going into business for myself. Maybe this is the time to do it. I've got some clients who would come with me. . . ." She paused and took a deep breath. "It's a really scary thought. I'd be completely on my own."

I encouraged Nora to stay with these thoughts, even though they made her uncomfortable. Once you have opened up a new thought-track through your associations to your daydreams, try to stay with it for a while. Nora struggled to "sit with"—not run away from—her anxiety about going out on her own. "My dad has always said I was pretty strong, that I helped him get through Mother's death. But I don't know if I could do it."

One day Nora told me, "You know what? Whether I go into business for myself or not, I'm living again. . . . I'm not focused on what's wrong with my body. I have some energy. . . ." And now she also had goals—new daydreams to give her life direction and herself a sense of hope about the future.

Nora's pain didn't suddenly disappear. Her relationships with her children remained stormy, although she felt she now had more of a handle on some of the issues involved. Her father continued to get worse. But her physical symptoms were no longer so frightening to her. When they occurred, she could use her daydreams to find the triggering concern—and, having done that, she could try to find a solution. It didn't always work—sometimes there simply wasn't a solution to be found—but, as Nora put it, "I don't panic about it every time something hurts or doesn't feel right anymore. I trust myself a little bit more. I can usually come up with a way to handle things—not perfectly, but at least well enough to keep going."

At times the organizing stories in our daydreams help us to understand why we are suffering. These explanations can help us cope with the pain, but sometimes they backfire, adding to, instead of alleviating, the hurt and fear they were supposed to explain away.

This is how it was for Dick.

TAKING IT PERSONALLY:
DAYDREAMS THAT ADD TO THE HURT

Dick was a short, rotund man with a cherubic face capped by tight gray curls. He was in his early fifties when I met him, less than a year after his wife, Cindi, had died of cancer.

"She was my second wife," he told me. "My first marriage, to my college sweetheart, was doomed from the beginning—although we tried hard to make it work. We got married because we goofed: she got pregnant when I was in my sophomore year. We lasted sixteen years and two more kids . . . and then I met Cindi." He paused, and when he started speaking again, his voice was husky. "Cindi was the love of my life. It's been nearly a year, and I still don't know how to live without her."

Dick took a deep breath. "I did fine the whole time Cindi was sick, and even for the first few months after . . . after she died. I mean, I guess I was in shock; but I managed to hold things together for all of us—Cindi and our daughter, Laurie, and myself.

"Now . . . it's almost a year. I shouldn't be so depressed. I should be getting over it by now. But . . . I've lost my whole life. I miss her so much. . . ." He choked back a sob.

After a moment, he continued: "If it hadn't been for Laurie, and the fact that she needed me, I would have killed myself. It would make things so much easier. I can't stand this roller coaster of feelings. Sometimes I feel so lost, and then other times I get so angry! I'm frightened of how *furious* I can get."

I asked Dick for an example. "Well, for starters, I think about suing the doctors or the hospital, although I know full well they did everything they possibly could. . . . And I get in a rage at

God. . . . I even get mad at Cindi. It seems to come over me all of a sudden, and I just snap. It's so bad at work that I'm worried about losing my job if I don't get it under control. But worse is that I'm doing it with Laurie, too. She's only thirteen, and she doesn't know how to deal with me when I get crazy angry. I don't know how to deal with me, either."

I told Dick that mourning is a process and that both depression and rage are normal reactions to the kind of loss he had suffered. I also encouraged him to let himself go through the process at his own pace, not according to some arbitrarily determined time schedule. "But," I added, "I understand that you need to have some control over your emotions so that you don't lose your job or cause emotional damage to your daughter." He sighed deeply as he nodded in agreement. "But how do I do that?" he asked.

I suggested that he start to keep track of his daydreams, particularly around the times he was filled with rage. "But I don't have any dreams anymore," he said. "They were all buried with Cindi."

I explained to him what I meant by "daydreams." "For example, you just told me that you have daydreams of suing the hospital or the doctors. And you have some sort of daydreams about expressing your fury to God and even to Cindi."

This idea captured his imagination. "You're right," he said. "I actually even imagine myself shaking my fist at God and dragging Cindi back from the dead—like Hercules brought back his friend's wife in Greek mythology."

It wasn't always easy for Dick, since the hostile feelings often seemed just to "take over," without any warning or reason. But as Dick struggled to keep track of these outbreaks and to find the daydream thoughts that preceded them, he learned some powerful information about his own thought processes.

"Here's one that keeps coming up," he told me. "I keep

asking myself why this had to happen to me. In fact, in her sermon at the funeral, our minister commented that it's a common response to the death of a loved one, but she said that it's the wrong question to ask—it happens to so many of us. She lost her husband just a few years ago, and she said there were many in the congregation who had also lost loved ones—husbands, wives, parents, children, brothers, sisters, lovers. . . . I don't remember what she said was the *right* question; I wasn't really paying much attention after that. But I think about it sometimes, because I do ask over and over again, 'Why me?'

"And here's what's really fascinating," he went on. "Since I've been keeping track of my daydreams—now that I know that I *have* them—I realize that I ask that question almost every time I start to get in a rage! Now, I don't know what it means, but it's got to mean something, right?"

I agreed that that was likely. Over time, as Dick continued to pay attention to his daydreams and associations, we learned at least one of the meanings of his question "Why me?"

"I went into a rage yesterday at work. A colleague had really screwed something up royally, and it was going to take us forever to straighten it out. I was so angry I could have chewed nails. But instead of blowing up, I made myself go into my office and write down every thought I could. I figured I'd get it out of my system on paper first . . . and maybe find out what some of my daydreams were, to boot. And here's what was so interesting. I must have written for about ten minutes, maybe less. I filled up three pages with writing. And at least fifty percent of what I said was, 'What did I do wrong? Why am I being punished like this?' "

I asked Dick to tell me what came to his mind concerning those words. "I've been thinking about that," he replied. "And what I keep coming up with is the thought that Cindi's death was my punishment for leaving my first wife and my kids." He paused. "I didn't do it very well. I just split—left 'em all. . . . I've felt guilty about it for a long time." He sighed. "Cindi really pushed me to rebuild a relationship with my kids, but it was hard. They were pretty mad at me—for good reason. And although they've been super during this time—my oldest girl, especially, has been great with Laurie—I've had thoughts, daydreams, that they must be feeling pleased that this happened to me. That I was finally getting my just reward."

Many of us organize painful episodes in a manner similar to Dick's—that is, by believing we're being punished or chosen to suffer by God or the Fates or some other entity. Or we may just decide that we have "bad luck," or that we're "jinxed." For most of us, as for Dick, these daydreams have multiple, sometimes contradictory meanings.

For example, Dick realized that these thoughts and daydreams predated Cindi's illness. "I've always felt responsible for anything bad that happens. You know—like I've brought these things on myself."

As Dick continued to keep a record of the words and thoughts that followed his daydreams, he noticed an interesting theme. "I keep using words that have to do with power and powerlessness. I think I can control what happens to me if I live the 'right' life. And when I can't, I get angry—and *that* makes me feel powerful, but only for a short time. Then I feel depleted and guilty. . . ." He stopped for a minute. "When I put those thoughts into words, I saw some of their flaws. First of all, it makes my pain worse, and that makes me angry. No wonder I lash out! But second of all, it's not the way the world works. I see plenty of other people suffering, and I don't think *they* deserve their misfortune. But when it's me, it's like I see every good thing as evidence that I'm good, and every bad thing as evidence that I'm bad. Like the fact that I had Laurie and Cindi in my life was proof that I was good; and Cindi's illness, that I'm bad." He paused thoughtfully. "I think like a little kid," he said slowly.

There was, of course, more to the picture. As Dick pursued his associations, he realized that this way of thinking was an attempt to protect himself from the unpredictability of life, which left him feeling vulnerable and raw. "I guess this way I feel safer— like there's a plan, or someone watching over me, giving things *order.*" But it also added to his burden and pain when things did not go well. Not only did he have to suffer from the loss itself, but he added to his pain by feeling that he had brought it on himself.

Recognizing these underlying stories did not make the painful loss of Cindi disappear. Dick still had to go through the mourning process, which was neither pleasant nor brief. But he found that his newfound knowledge helped him manage the painful, powerful, and sometimes intolerable feelings that are part of mourning.

As he continued to track his daydreams and the thoughts that followed them over time, he made still other discoveries about himself. For example, one day as Dick began to talk about his and Laurie's vacation plans, he burst into tears. "I . . . I just realized that I'm planning to have a good time *without* Cindi." He was starting to see that even burgeoning, hopeful daydreams about the future could cause him pain. "I feel guilty, as though I'm leaving her behind . . . as though she doesn't really mean so much to me. . . ."

Dick would have to learn to tolerate the experience of pleasure without Cindi; and he would have to find a way to allow himself to grow, knowing that Cindi could no longer do so.

His daydreams were a powerful source of information in the process. One day he said, sadly, "I've just begun to see that I have to find a place to keep the memories, without feeling like I have to stay buried with Cindi—stay back in the time I spent with her. Laurie and I started that process yesterday by looking at some old photos of Cindi and the two of us. We both cried, but we talked about how important those memories were, and how important it was to try to keep them and move on from them at the same time. . . . I started to see that those memories are like daydreams—part of me, but not all of me. I'm not sure how to make it work, but at least I have an idea now."

Although the word "play" may seem too light for the mourning process, it was exactly what Dick was doing—and what he was teaching Laurie to do. Memories are daydreams. And daydreams are not static. If you can "play" with them—change, add, subtract details, make them looser and more free-flowing—appreciate them, and explore them, they will more easily come and go, and you won't get stuck in them. They will always be part of your experience, but with more intensity at some times than at others. And they will become part of your life and who you are, instead of ruts you get stuck in or obstacles that impede your progress.

In the next story, you will see how a couple got stuck in their daydreams, and how they learned to "play" with them. And you will see how they learned not only to cope with their pain, but to use their daydreams to connect with each other, to enhance their relationship so that they could struggle through their pain together.

"WE WANT A BABY": HOW SHARED DAYDREAMS CAN HURT—OR HELP—A RELATIONSHIP

Sam was forty-five and Lisa nearly forty when I met them. They were both of medium height, with dark, wavy hair, good-looking, and athletic. They told me that they were both avid tennis players and had met and fallen in love at a tennis camp nearly ten years earlier. In our first meeting, they could talk about only one thing: their daydreams of the family they could not have.

They had been trying to get pregnant for over four years.

After a variety of treatments, they had gone through two cycles of *in vitro* fertilization. They were trying to decide whether to continue the costly and time-consuming process, or to begin adoption procedures. "Although," Sam said, "we've heard such horror stories about *that* process: birth mothers changing their minds at the last minute, or selling the baby to a higher bidder after you've paid for her medical treatment and care for the past nine months; months spent in South America or China or other countries trying to get a baby out. . . . I'm not sure I've got the emotional or financial wherewithal for that, either."

"We could try to get pregnant on our own for a cycle or two while we're making up our minds," Lisa said, "but . . ."

"But we have another problem," Sam interjected. He looked down, embarrassed. "I can't keep an erection."

Lisa tried to be reassuring. "It's not your fault, honey." Turning to me, she said, "We saw a sex therapist, who said that it's a normal reaction to infertility. She gave us some exercises, but the thing is, Sam won't even try them. We're supposed to do something romantic, or cuddle up with each other and enjoy being physical, but without doing anything sexual. He gets angry if I even bring up the subject. We don't even try anymore." She began to cry. Sam slipped a furtive look in her direction, but said nothing.

I told them that I knew this was a difficult process and that, though I didn't want to bring up unpleasant feelings unnecessarily, I wondered if they would be willing to talk about some of their daydreams about having a baby. "You probably think about these things anyway," I said gently. "And your daydreams might give us some important clues to what's going on."

"Well," Sam said, "I guess that's what I'm here for. But be prepared, I may start to cry. Talking about it does that to me." He took a deep breath. "I have lots of ideas about what it would be like to have a child," he said. "Is that what you mean by daydreams?"

"Exactly," I replied.

"Okay. I imagine myself holding a baby, rocking him in my arms. My friends with kids tell me I'm nuts, but I even think it would be great to wake up in the middle of the night. I figure Lisa would pump her milk so that I could do the night feeding, so I could 'bond' with the baby and let Lisa get some sleep. I imagine holding him, sitting in our big easy chair, giving him the bottle." He stopped for a moment. "I keep calling the baby 'him,' " he said. "Does that have any meaning?"

I said it might: "Do you particularly want a boy?"

"I'd be thrilled with a girl *or* a boy," he replied, "but it is true that most of my daydreams are about a boy. I guess it's the male-bonding thing. I think about playing baseball with my son . . . teaching him to play tennis . . . watching the NCAA tournament with him. . . ."

Tears began to form in his eyes. Lisa reached out and took Sam's hand. He sniffed, patted her hand, pulled his away. Lisa, too, began to cry. "This kind of thing happens all the time now," she said to me through her tears. "I'm beginning to think that the real reason we don't make love is that Sam doesn't find me attractive. Once he couldn't keep his hands off me. Now it seems like he doesn't want to touch me at all."

I explained to them that that was one of *her* daydreams—a painful one—and that one of our tasks was to sort out how these daydreams were related to their difficulties.

"I don't know if it's a daydream," Sam interjected. "I mean, I'm not sure anymore what's me and what's Lisa. It is true that I don't want her to touch me most of the time now."

Lisa looked upset. "That's what I thought," she said. "Now what?"

I said that because of all the stress they were experiencing, it was too early to tell if this symptom was reflective of a permanent change in Sam's feelings about Lisa. I asked them both to try to keep a record of the times when Sam didn't want Lisa to touch him: what they were doing, talking about, thinking, and feeling. And I suggested they look for any themes or patterns that started to appear. Within a few days, they had noticed one basic pattern. Sam said, "Every time Lisa touches me these days, it seems to stir up my feelings of inadequacy. I can't make a baby, and I can't make love. Even when she tries to comfort me, like she did just now, I feel like it's because I'm such a failure—a real weakling. For Christ's sake, I'm a full-grown man and I start to *cry* when I think about holding my own baby or taking my son to a ball game. I guess her touch reminds me that I don't feel very manly these days."

Sam's assumption that Lisa's and his inability to have a child was a direct reflection on his masculinity contributed to a vicious cycle: as he questioned his masculinity, he found himself having difficulties maintaining an erection, which then underscored his feelings of inadequacy. His daydreams about a boy baby, with whom he would do "man things," was in part an unconscious attempt to compensate for that feeling of not being a "real" man. But it also reflected his belief that he would be truly manly only if he could create a baby. With his feelings of inadequacy reinforced, he began to avoid sex. Eventually he stopped all physical contact with Lisa, because whenever he became aroused he also became anxious about not being able to perform sexually.

But, as usual, this wasn't the whole story. Lisa's response, which was to be concerned and maternal, also felt condescending to Sam, and this added further to his feelings of not being a real man.

Lisa's reaction surprised—and interested—Sam.

"My God," she said, "you're so masculine. I can't believe you feel that way." And then it hit her. "But I *do* understand! Because I have the same kind of feelings about myself. There are lots of things about having a baby that I long for. I want to feel special in that way that you can only feel if you're somebody's mommy. And I've always thought that I would feel *complete* when I had a family. But I never thought what 'complete' meant. I guess one of the things it means is . . . that I would be a real woman." Tears filled her eyes. "I knew I'd been feeling like I wasn't attractive to Sam anymore, but I didn't realize that I was actually interpreting his lack of interest in sex as a response to my inadequacies as a woman. And yet I have had thoughts—daydreams, I guess you'd say—that, because my female organs aren't working, I'm a failure as a woman. I'm not able to do what I was biologically created to do."

These realizations did not stop the hurt, and they did not miraculously make Sam able to keep an erection. But Sam and Lisa had discovered that their pain was increased by the unspoken assumptions they had in common that their inability to conceive was a reflection of their worth as a man or a woman rather than as a painful piece of bad luck that they shared.

Having put this daydream into words for the first time, Sam and Lisa found themselves able to take yet another step in the mourning process. Mourning, like every other emotional phenomenon we have talked about in this book, is a *process;* it has more than one component—it changes and encompasses many (sometimes contradictory) feelings. In order to move on with our lives, we have to go through all of what the process entails. Naturally, because it can be so painful, we often look for ways around it; but sometimes the very ways we find to bypass the feelings keep us stuck in the agony we're trying to avoid.

Lisa and Sam now saw that the shame they had both buried in their daydreams had had a significant impact on their relationship. As they shared their daydreams with one another and began to question the unexamined assumptions the daydreams contained, the couple opened new avenues for discussion and exploration.

"Every month we get all built up; and every month we have

a terrible loss," Sam said. "Don't let anyone tell you that you can only feel that loss when a real baby dies. We lose everything each month: our hopes, our dreams, our self-confidence, our trust in the world, and the baby we've been imagining starting to grow in Lisa's womb." He was silent for a moment, scuffing one foot against the floor a few times; then he looked at me. "You know," he said slowly, "you don't ever fully mourn while this is going on. . . . You get so caught up in the cycle, because, seven days after you find out that you don't have a baby, you start all over again."

Lisa seemed to understand. "So, Sam, maybe you've been trying to tell us something," she said. Sam turned and looked directly at her. "Maybe . . . maybe we've got to stop and mourn our losses, not just try to deny them," she continued. "We've got to really face what's going on here. That"—her voice caught, but she went on—"that we aren't going to have our own baby."

Once again, putting this thought into words did not end their struggle, either to have a baby or to mourn their losses. It was one more association and one more daydream, but only one of many. The process was not easy; nor was it a simple matter to get their relationship back on firm ground. But as Sam and Lisa allowed themselves to talk about their pain, their feelings of mourning, rage, and hurt, something occurred that neither of them expected.

Sam remembered that one of the specialists he had consulted had suggested a new treatment that would not improve their ability to conceive but would make it possible for them to have intercourse: a hormone that, when injected, would give him an erection. "I had completely forgotten the whole thing," he said in amazement. "I guess I really needed to pay attention to the difficult stuff I'd been trying to block out—and to open up what's

going on in our relationship—before I could remember it."
Through his doctor, he now obtained the hormone. The emotional pain was not gone; and intimacy was a sometimes fragile,
often tentative new experience. But he and Lisa were, finally, a bit
more hopeful about their future. "If we can remember to talk to
each other—to really talk—at least there may be a chance for our
relationship," Lisa said. And Sam added, "We've been so focused
on making a baby that we haven't paid attention to that. I wanted
to have a baby with Lisa because I love her. The crucial thing
right now is to see if we can get our relationship back on track—
baby or no baby."

Loss, and the mourning that goes along with it, is not just
one emotion, but a complex mixture of feelings and thoughts.
And it is a different experience each time we go through it,
although each time may carry with it themes and threads from
previous losses. It is also different for each of us: how we deal with
and ultimately even experience loss depends on many other factors, including how we organize the experience itself.

It isn't always easy to explore—even to find—your daydreams when you are in pain. They are there, but sometimes they
hurt so much that you bury them deeper than usual; or you feel so
lost you can't begin to look inside yourself—even to begin
making any associations. This is a normal reaction to severe pain
and traumatic loss: we seem to shut down, closing off to protect
ourselves from overwhelming and unprocessed emotion.

Mourning—like every other cluster of feelings—is a personal experience. Your way is not wrong just because it is different. Try not to put yourself down for your thoughts, feelings,
or images. No one can tell you how or when or even whom or
what to mourn. For some of us, for example, the loss of a beloved
pet is highly traumatic, whereas for others it is only a little sad.

The loss of a home can be extremely painful to one person and nearly meaningless to another. A divorce, even from a despised spouse, can turn from relief to loss for one person, from loss to joy for someone else.

As you think about your own ways of dealing with loss, think, too, about how you interpret—or explain—your experience. Cull your daydreams for this information, using some of the tools you've acquired in earlier chapters. But if you are in mourning and your daydreams aren't yet available to you, don't worry. Respect your own needs and allow yourself to go at your own pace. If you make the space and time, you will eventually begin to daydream again—and when you are ready, the following exercise will help you use these daydreams to cope with your loss, and to move on.

EXERCISE:

DEALING WITH "BAD" FEELINGS

1. If something is making you feel bad—whether it is a painful loss, a hurtful comment, a self-criticism—start by describing just what has happened. Say it out loud, to yourself; or tell a friend. Or write a few sentences about it in your diary.

For example, Henry was in his fifties when his company downsized and he was fired for the first time in his life. Despite a really good "package," he wasn't able to get over the pain of the experience. This is what he wrote:

I've worked for this company for twenty-five years. Then they fire me. How could they do this? What's this world coming to? What the hell am I going to do?

2. Look for the kind of key words and phrases we've talked about: any that convey strong feelings and any that have obvious associations for you. Write these words down, too.

Your sentences, like Henry's, may not have any "feeling" words in them but, also like his, they may convey emotion; if so, write those feelings down. Henry wrote "anger, resentment, fear, disappointment."

3. Now think of any other times you've felt this way. What have you done those times? How have you coped with the feelings? Do any of your old solutions work for you now?

4. Look for themes in your coping style. Ask yourself what stories—assumptions—these solutions convey. What are you trying to accomplish with these stories? Is your goal being achieved?

Again, don't stop with the obvious or the easy. Push the envelope. See what *else* these daydreams are telling you.

Loss is an inevitable part of life. Although we try to avoid it or dilute it in many ways, we cannot get away from it. Mourning is a painful but also productive response to loss. We mourn what no longer exists, what never will be, what never was. But as we have seen, other feelings are also "normal" responses to loss: sadness and pain, naturally, but also rage, shame, guilt, disappointment, longing, the whole gamut of human emotion.

If you are stuck in your pain, unable to do the work of mourning, to move through and beyond it, you are probably also unable to feel the joys that can still be part of your life—even after devastating loss. This is not to say that the pain will go away forever. Some pain—the death of a child, for example, or your own aching wish that you had had a better childhood—may always be in the background (and at times in the foreground) of your experience for the rest of your life.

Your daydreams can keep you tied to the pain, or, with a little effort, you can turn the prism: you can use these daily imaginings to help you gain more perspective about your motives, about how your daydreams are serving your psyche. If you do, you will not find Never Never Land; you won't live happily ever after; but you will find some of the richly elaborate experience that life has to offer. You will be able to move on with more confidence, self-awareness, and hope.

2. Look for the kind of key words and phrases we've talked about: any that convey strong feelings and any that have obvious associations for you. Write these words down, too.

Your sentences, like Henry's, may not have any "feeling" words in them but, also like his, they may convey emotion; if so, write those feelings down. Henry wrote "anger, resentment, fear, disappointment."

3. Now think of any other times you've felt this way. What have you done those times? How have you coped with the feelings? Do any of your old solutions work for you now?

4. Look for themes in your coping style. Ask yourself what stories—assumptions—these solutions convey. What are you trying to accomplish with these stories? Is your goal being achieved?

Again, don't stop with the obvious or the easy. Push the envelope. See what *else* these daydreams are telling you.

Loss is an inevitable part of life. Although we try to avoid it or dilute it in many ways, we cannot get away from it. Mourning is a painful but also productive response to loss. We mourn what no longer exists, what never will be, what never was. But as we have seen, other feelings are also "normal" responses to loss: sadness and pain, naturally, but also rage, shame, guilt, disappointment, longing, the whole gamut of human emotion.

If you are stuck in your pain, unable to do the work of mourning, to move through and beyond it, you are probably also unable to feel the joys that can still be part of your life—even after devastating loss. This is not to say that the pain will go away forever. Some pain—the death of a child, for example, or your own aching wish that you had had a better childhood—may always be in the background (and at times in the foreground) of your experience for the rest of your life.

Your daydreams can keep you tied to the pain, or, with a little effort, you can turn the prism: you can use these daily imaginings to help you gain more perspective about your motives, about how your daydreams are serving your psyche. If you do, you will not find Never Never Land; you won't live happily ever after; but you will find some of the richly elaborate experience that life has to offer. You will be able to move on with more confidence, self-awareness, and hope.

CHAPTER TEN

Precious Jewels:
Dream On!

W E HAVE COME to the end of our journey together into the world of your daydreams. But although this is the last chapter of the book, it is far from the end of your personal odyssey. You have just begun the incredible visit to your internal world and the self-awareness it brings. Don't stop now. Continue exploring your daydreams and pursuing the thoughts and associations that accompany them to find out more about yourself, to expand your horizons, to help you live the life of your dreams.

A meditation for the Jewish Sabbath service begins, "I harbor within . . . a vision of my highest self, a dream of what I could and should become." That dream can be a tool in your quest to live a rich and honest life, to be a good and caring person, to reach your most prized goals; but it can also backfire, causing pain and misery, if you can only view it literally, as a "should" instead of a wish. In truth, we all harbor many different visions of ourselves—not just our highest, but also our lowest selves; selves we long to be, and selves we wish we had been; selves we prefer to hide, and selves we want to show the world. As you put these visions of yourself into words, you will add to your self-knowledge and your capacity to grow and change; as a result, you will broaden your sense of the *choices* in your life.

You've learned that your daydreams are *not* trivial fragments of thought floating through your overloaded mind, nor are they meaningless distractions that interfere with your ability to focus. Whether snippets of ideas or full-blown stories, whether fantastical wishes or realistic plans, you now know that your daydreams are extremely relevant. *They have meaning.* And as you mine them for the precious gems they contain, you gain insight into how you organize and (without always consciously realizing it) build your own experience.

By reading the stories, doing the exercises, and asking yourself some of the questions I raise in each chapter, you have been building a growing understanding of yourself. You have been strengthening your fantasy "muscles," and collecting tools that aid you in your quest to discover and polish the jewels of self-knowledge reflected in your daydreams.

And you have most likely encountered moments—maybe days, or even weeks—when you closed this book, put down your daydream journal, and stopped playing with your daydreams. Did you wonder why? The answer is deceptively simple. Fantasy can be risky. It can open up worlds that you've spent a lifetime closing down, keeping at a distance. Exploring this realm disrupts your security and safety.

You are not an inadequate, lazy, or cowardly person if this happens to you. In fact, one of the lessons we've learned from pursuing daydreams is that it is important—crucial, in fact—to take this journey at your own pace, to respect your own resistances. Go slowly—*stop,* even—when you need to, and then romp along at a riotous pace when you feel like it. As you develop your own rhythm of self-exploration, you will find yourself thinking and writing about, and making space in your life for, powerful emotions like love and affection, passion and excitement, anger, sadness, and—yes—a far more rooted security and safety. The more you understand about yourself, the more you open up the range of possibilities in your life. Without always knowing it, you have widened your choices and increased your ability to make decisions, both large and small.

Daydreams connect past, present, and future in ways we cannot always foretell. They fill in gaps, offer solace, provide explanations. They are full of unrecognized assumptions. They contain memories and plans, hopes and fears, sadness and happiness, rage and sympathy, and so much more—all the emotions and experiences of your own richly human life.

You can continue to use *Daydreaming* as a guide to your ongoing exploration of the universe of your daydreams. Now that you've read through the entire book, you may want to turn to specific chapters to refresh your memory and focus on particularly compelling, confusing, or difficult areas. Go back and do the exercises as many times as you please. Don't be surprised if you find something completely different each time you do an exercise, or find yourself drawn to an exercise you weren't interested in last time around. Try not to limit yourself or close off your options.

Look at the same chapters from a different perspective—whatever perspective your current circumstances or feelings encourage you to take.

Remember, this won't result in any "finished product" or unchanging facts about yourself. Your daydreams are as ongoing as you are. Sometimes they keep things the same; sometimes they allow (even help) you to choose. Reread the chapters, redo the exercises—shift the prism ever so slightly, see what you find, and allow the landscape of your life to widen.

FURTHER READING ON DAYDREAMS

A NUMBER OF books and articles were extremely useful to me in the writing of this book. If you would like to do some further reading in this area, here are some suggestions.

Casey, Edward S. *Imagining*. Bloomington: Indiana University Press, 1979.

Pope, Kenneth S., and Jerome L. Singer, eds. *The Stream of Consciousness*. New York: Plenum Press, 1978.

Singer, Jerome L. *The Inner World of Daydreaming*. New York: Harper Colophon, 1975.

Wolman, Benjamin B., ed. *Handbook of Dreams*. New York: Van Nostrand Reinhold Co., 1979.